J. Parker Norris

The Portraits of Shakespeare

J. Parker Norris

The Portraits of Shakespeare

ISBN/EAN: 9783337063085

Printed in Europe, USA, Canada, Australia, Japan

Cover: Foto ©ninafisch / pixelio.de

More available books at **www.hansebooks.com**

THE PORTRAITS

OF

SHAKESPEARE

THE

PORTRAITS OF SHAKESPEARE

BY

J. PARKER NORRIS

"Look here, upon this picture, and on this."—Hamlet, III, iv, 53

PHILADELPHIA
ROBERT M. LINDSAY
1885

Press of Globe Printing House
Philadelphia

TO

HORACE HOWARD FURNESS, Ph.D., LL.D.

THIS BOOK IS AFFECTIONATELY DEDICATED

BY HIS FRIEND

J. PARKER NORRIS

PREFACE.

THE list of books consulted in the preparation of this volume will give a fair idea of the mass of literature which has accumulated around the portraits of Shakespeare. Three books, however, stand prominently forth—Boaden's *Inquiry*, 1824, Wivell's *Inquiry*, 1827, and Friswell's *Life Portraits*, 1864.

The excellence of Boaden's work is marred by its diffuse style. He seems to have endeavored to fill out his book by the insertion of matter which is foreign to his subject, and even in the discussion of the traits of a portrait his many words obscure his meaning.

Wivell's book is a literary curiosity. He was evidently a wholly uneducated man, and his style is turgid in the extreme. He reprinted much of Boaden's material, but he also added interesting descriptions of portraits passed over by his predecessor. He was untiring in his labors, and had the advantage, withal, of being himself a portrait painter. Doubtless had he been able to endow his purposes with words his work would have been peculiarly valuable.

Friswell had the advantage of the labors of Boaden and Wivell, and of new material which had come to light since their day. His book unfortunately bears evidence of hasty preparation, and contains numerous errors revealing the lack of thorough study.

While thus discussing his predecessors who have so bravely tried to knit into one fair pattern the ravelled sleeve gathered from many hands, let not ingratitude be imputed to the present writer. He has often had occasion to avail himself of their labors, and care has always been taken to duly acknowledge the debt. Every available source of information has been searched, and whatsoever is known on this subject is here presented. All that is claimed for this work is a careful collection of all information from every source.

The pleasant duty remains of acknowledging the assistance which has been extended to him by George Adam Burn, Esq., Horace Howard Furness, Ph.D., LL.D., C. M. Ingleby, LL.D., Gen. Charles K. Loring, Isaac Norris, M.D., John Rabone, Esq., Albert H. Smyth, Esq., and Samuel Timmins, Esq., J. P., to all of whom he is very grateful.

CONTENTS.

	PAGE
SHALL WE OPEN SHAKESPEARE'S GRAVE? A PLEA FOR ASCERTAINING THE TRUE LIKENESS OF THE POET	1
THE STRATFORD BUST	21
THE DROESHOUT ENGRAVING	45
THE CHANDOS PORTRAIT	67
THE DEATH MASK	93
THE JANSEN PORTRAIT	122
THE FELTON PORTRAIT	141
THE STRATFORD PORTRAIT	153
THE ASHBORNE PORTRAIT	166
THE DUKE OF DEVONSHIRE BUST	172
THE HAMPTON COURT PORTRAIT	179
THE HILLIARD MINIATURE	182
THE WARWICK PORTRAIT	187
THE JENNINGS MINIATURE	189
THE BURN PORTRAIT	191
THE LUMLEY PORTRAIT	192
THE BOSTON ART MUSEUM PORTRAIT	196
THE CHALLIS PORTRAIT	199

CONTENTS.

THE ZOUST PORTRAIT	201
THE ZUCCHERO PORTRAIT	204
THE BOARDMAN MINIATURE	206
THE STACE PORTRAIT	208
THE O'CONNELL PORTRAIT	210
THE GILLILAND PORTRAIT	211
THE HARDIE PORTRAIT	213
THE LIDDELL PORTRAIT	215
THE DUNFORD PORTRAIT	218
THE WINSTANLEY PORTRAIT	224
THE ZINCKE PORTRAIT	226
THE TALMA PORTRAIT	228
THE MONUMENT IN WESTMINSTER ABBEY	230
THE SHAKESPEARE GALLERY ALTO RELIEVO	232
THE ROUBILIAC STATUE	234
THE WARD STATUE	235

LIST OF ILLUSTRATIONS.

	PAGE
PAGE'S BUST. FROM CRAYON DRAWING OF ORIGINAL.	FRONTISPIECE.
THE STRATFORD BUST. FROM PHOTOGRAPH OF ORIGINAL BY THRUPP. (LARGE VIEW.)	21
THE STRATFORD BUST. FROM PHOTOGRAPH OF ORIGINAL BY THRUPP. (SMALLER VIEW, SHOWING THE WHOLE MONUMENT.)	27
THE STRATFORD BUST. FROM PHOTOGRAPH OF ORIGINAL.	37
THE DROESHOUT ENGRAVING. FROM PHOTO-LITHOGRAPH OF ORIGINAL BY DAY & SON, FROM THE EARL OF ELLESMERE'S COPY.	45
THE TITLE-PAGE OF THE FIRST FOLIO EDITION OF SHAKESPEARE, SHOWING THE MANNER IN WHICH THE DROESHOUT ENGRAVING APPEARED IN THAT VOLUME.	47
MARSHALL'S COPY OF THE DROESHOUT ENGRAVING. FROM AN OLD PRINT (ENGRAVER'S NAME UNKNOWN.)	59
THE CHANDOS PORTRAIT. FROM MEZZOTINT BY SAMUEL COUSINS.	67
THE DEATH MASK. FROM PHOTOGRAPH OF ORIGINAL BY WILLIAM PAGE. (PROFILE.)	93

LIST OF ILLUSTRATIONS.

The Death Mask. From Photograph of original by William Page. (Three-quarter face view.) . . . 95

The Death Mask. From Photographs of original. (Four small views, showing the Mask in different positions.) 97

The Kesselstadt Picture. From Photograph of original. 99

The Jansen Portrait. From Mezzotint by Charles Turner. 123

The Felton Portrait. From Engraving by T. Trotter. (The small square shows the actual condition of the picture. The portion of the plate in outline is supplied from the Droeshout Engraving.) 141

The Felton Portrait. From Engraving by T. Trotter. (The dress restored from the Droeshout Engraving.) 145

The Stratford Portrait. From Photograph of original by Cundall, Downes, & Co. . . 153

The Stratford Portrait. From Photograph of original. 163

The Ashborne Portrait. From Mezzotint by G. F. Storm. 167

The Duke of Devonshire Bust. From Photograph of original. 173

The Hilliard Miniature. From Engraving by T. W. Harland. 183

LIST OF ILLUSTRATIONS.

THE JENNINGS MINIATURE. FROM ENGRAVING BY W. HOLL.	189
THE BURN PORTRAIT. FROM PHOTOGRAPH OF ORIGINAL.	191
THE BOSTON ART MUSEUM PORTRAIT. FROM PHOTOGRAPH OF ORIGINAL BY SONREL.	197
THE ZOUST PORTRAIT. FROM ENGRAVING BY W. HOLL.	201
THE ZUCCHERO PORTRAIT. FROM ENGRAVING BY W. HOLL.	205
THE STACE PORTRAIT. FROM ENGRAVING BY W. HOLL.	209
THE GILLILAND PORTRAIT. FROM ENGRAVING BY W. HOLL.	211
THE DUNFORD PORTRAIT. FROM ENGRAVING BY W. SHARP.	219
THE ZINCKE PORTRAIT. FROM ENGRAVING BY W. HOLL.	227
THE MONUMENT IN WESTMINSTER ABBEY. FROM ENGRAVING BY B. HOLL.	231
THE SHAKESPEARE GALLERY ALTO-RELIEVO. FROM ENGRAVING BY B. HOLL.	233
THE ROUBILIAC STATUE. FROM ENGRAVING BY W. HOLL.	234
THE WARD STATUE. FROM PHOTOGRAPH OF ORIGINAL BY ROCKWOOD.	235

LIST OF BOOKS, MAGAZINE AND NEWSPAPER ARTICLES, ETC., CONSULTED IN THE PREPARATION OF THIS VOLUME.

[JENNENS, CHARLES:] The Tragedy of *King Lear*, as lately published, Vindicated from the Abuse of the Critical Reviewers; and the Wonderful Genius and Abilities of those Gentlemen for Criticism, set forth, celebrated, and extolled, by the Editor of *King Lear*. 8vo. London: 1772.

[STEEVENS, GEORGE:] Proposals by William Richardson, Printseller, etc., for the publication of the Felton Portrait of Shakespeare. With Supplement. 8vo. London: 1794.

[BRITTON, JOHN:] Remarks on the Monumental Bust of Shakespeare, at Stratford-upon-Avon, etc. 8vo. London: 1816.

BOADEN, JAMES: An Inquiry into the Authenticity of various Pictures and Prints, which, from the decease of the Poet to our own times, have been offered to the public as portraits of Shakespeare, etc. 8vo. London: 1824.

BOADEN, JAMES: An Inquiry into the Authenticity of various Pictures and Prints, which, from the decease of the Poet to our own times, have been offered to the public as portraits of Shakespeare, etc. [This is sometimes called a large paper edition of the former book, but it is not, for the type is entirely reset, and the page made a quarto thereby—not by merely adding margin as in large paper copies. The illustrations are the same as in the former, but are India paper proofs.] 4to. London: 1824.

WIVELL, ABRAHAM: An Historical Account of the Monumental Bust of William Shakespeare, in the Chancel of the Church, at Stratford-upon-Avon, etc. 8vo. London: 1827.

WIVELL, ABRAHAM: An Inquiry into the History, Authenticity, and Characteristics of the Shakespeare Portraits, etc. 8vo. London: 1827.

WIVELL, ABRAHAM: A Supplement to an Inquiry into the History, Authenticity, and Characteristics of the Shakespeare Portraits, etc. 8vo. London: 1827.

[WILSON, JOHN:] Shakespeariana. Catalogue of all the books, pamphlets, etc., relating to Shakespeare, etc. 16mo. London: 1827.

WIVELL, ABRAHAM: An Inquiry into the History, Authenticity, and Characteristics of the Shakespeare Portraits, etc. 8vo. London: 1840.

LIST OF BOOKS, ETC. xvii

HALLIWELL–PHILLIPPS, J. O.: The Life of William Shakespeare. 8vo. London: 1848.

WALPOLE, HORACE: Anecdotes of Painting. Edited by Ralph N. Wornum. 8vo. London: 1849.

FORSTER, HENRY RUMSEY: A Few Remarks by Henry Rumsey Forster on the Chandos Portrait of Shakespeare, etc. [Privately printed.] 8vo. London: 1849.

ANONYMOUS: The Chandos Portrait of Shakespeare. [Apparently a privately issued reprint of articles on the Chandos Portrait contributed to *The Athenæum* and *The Literary Gazette*. It has no title-page, or date of publication.] 8vo. [London: 1849?]

BRITTON, JOHN: Appendix to Britton's Auto-Biography, etc. 8vo. London: 1850.

HALLIWELL–PHILLIPPS, J. O.: The Works of William Shakespeare. [Folio Edition. Vol. I. One hundred and fifty copies printed.] Folio. London: 1853.

WAAGEN, GUSTAV FRIEDRICH: Treasures of Art in Great Britain. Vol. III. 8vo. London: 1854.

WRIGHT, CHARLES: The Stratford Portrait of Shakespeare, and *The Athenæum*, etc. [No title-page.] 8vo. London: 1861.

WRIGHT, CHARLES: The Stratford Portrait of Shakespeare. Copies of Communications to *The Times*, etc. [No title-page.] London: 1861.

WRIGHT, CHARLES: Shakespeare and Ben Jonson, etc. [No title-page. Privately printed.] 8vo. London: 1861.

BOHN, HENRY G.: Lowndes' Bibliographer's Manual, etc. 12mo. London: 1863.

ANONYMOUS: Shakespeare Portraits. [In *The Leisure Hour* for April 23, 1864.] Royal 8vo. London: 1864.

THOMS, WILLIAM J.: The Stratford Bust of Shakespeare. [In *Notes and Queries* for March 19, 1864.] 4to. London: 1864.

SCHARF, GEORGE: On the Principal Portraits of Shakespeare. [In *Notes and Queries* for April 23, 1864.] London: 1864.

NEIL, SAMUEL: Jonson's Lines on Shakespeare's Portrait. [In *Notes and Queries* for April 23, 1864.] London: 1864.

THOMS, WILLIAM J.: The Kesselstadt Mask of Shakespeare. [In *Notes and Queries* for April 23, 1864.] London: 1864.

ANONYMOUS: Shakespeare's Portraits. [In *Notes and Queries* for May 21, 1864.] London: 1864.

SCHARF, GEORGE: On the Principal Portraits of Shakespeare. [Reprinted from *Notes and Queries*.] 32mo. London: 1864.

FRISWELL, J. HAIN: Life Portraits of William Shakespeare, etc. 8vo. London: 1864.

CRAIG, E. T.: The Portraits, Bust, and Monument of Shakespeare. [Part II. of this work is entitled: *Shakespeare: or the Ardens of Warwickshire, and the Heritage of Genius.*] 16mo. London: [1864?]

ANONYMOUS: Catalogue of Pictures and Drawings exhibited at the Town Hall, Stratford-upon-Avon, at the celebration of the Tercentenary Birthday of William Shakespeare. 16mo. London: 1864.

HARRISON, GABRIEL: The Stratford Bust of William Shakespeare, etc. [Privately printed.] 4to. Brooklyn: 1865.

ELZE, K.: Shakespeare's Portraits. [In *Jahrbuch* of German Shakespeare Society for 1867.] 8vo. Berlin: 1867.

GRIMM, HERMANN: Shakespeare's Todtenmaske. [In *Über Künstler und Kunstwerke*.] 8vo. Berlin: 1867.

HALLIWELL–PHILLIPPS, J. O.: A Catalogue of a small portion of the Engravings and Drawings Illustrative of the Life of Shakespeare, preserved in the collection formed by J. O. Halliwell, Esq., F.R.S., etc. [Privately printed.] 8vo. London: 1868.

CARTER, SUSAN NICHOLS: The President of the National Academy. [A sketch of William Page, and an account of his copy from the Death Mask. In *Appleton's Journal* for December 2, 1871.] New York: 1871.

STODDARD, R. H.: Shakespeare Portraits. [In *The Aldine* for May, 1872.] New York: 1872.

ANONYMOUS: Ward's Statue of Shakespeare. [In *Atlantic Monthly* for September, 1872.] Boston: 1872.

HOLDER, H. W.: The Marriage of Shakespeare. [Reprinted from *The Scarborough Gazette*, 1873.] 8vo. Scarborough: 1873.

WRIGHT, H.: Shakespeare's Portraits. [In *The Antiquary* for November 8, 1873.] London: 1873.

MALAM, JOHN: The Shakespeare Marriage Picture, etc. 16mo. London: 1873.

ANONYMOUS: Shakespeare's Death Mask. [In *The New York Herald* for November 10, 1873.] New York: 1873.

ANONYMOUS: The Face of Shakespeare. [In *Evening Post* for November 15, 1873.] New York: 1873.

NORRIS, J. PARKER: The Various Portraits of Shakespeare. [In *The Evening Telegraph* for November 17, 1873.] Philadelphia: 1873.

ANONYMOUS: Mr. Page on Shakespeare. [In *The Evening Post.*] New York: 1873.

ANONYMOUS: The Portraits of Shakespeare. [In *The Chronicle* for November 19, 1873.] Germantown: 1873.

ANONYMOUS: Mr. Page's Mask of Shakespeare. [In *The New York Tribune* for November 28, 1873.] New York: 1873.

ANONYMOUS: Shakespeare. Ward's Statue in Central Park. [Privately printed.] Royal 8vo. New York: 1873.

O'DONOVAN, WILLIAM R.: A Statue of Shakespeare. [In *Lippincott's Magazine* for January, 1874.] Philadelphia: 1874.

GRAY, CHARLES G.: Shakespeare's Scar. [In *The New York Tribune*, May, 1874.] New York: 1874.

ANONYMOUS: Evidence for the Existence of the Scar. [In *The New York Tribune*, May, 1874.] New York: 1874.

ANONYMOUS: Pictures at the Academy. [In *The Home Journal* for May 20, 1874.] New York: 1874.

ANONYMOUS: The Death Mask of Shakespeare. [In *The Sunday Dispatch* for June 21, 1874.] Philadelphia: 1874.

HART, JOHN S.: The Shakespeare Death Mask. [In *Scribner's Monthly* for July, 1874.] New York: 1874.

ANONYMOUS: The Death Mask. [In *The Morning Advertiser* for July 11, 1874.] London: 1874.

ANONYMOUS: The Death Mask. [In *The Nation*, August, 1874.] New York: 1874.

ANONYMOUS: The Death Mask of Shakespeare. [In *The New York Herald* for September 28, 1874.] New York: 1874.

ANONYMOUS: The Shakespearian Portraits. Opinions of Scholars upon the celebrated Death Mask, etc. [In *The New York Herald* for September 28, 1874.] New York: 1874.

ANONYMOUS: The Mask of Shakespeare. [In *The New York Tribune* for November 15, 1874.] New York: 1874.

ANONYMOUS: The Lumley Portrait of Shakespeare. [No title-page.] 8vo. London: 1874.

CRAIG, E. T.: Shakespeare's Portraits Phrenologically Considered. [Originally published in an English journal April 30, 1864, and now privately reprinted.] 8vo. Philadelphia: 1875.

NORRIS, J. PARKER: The Death Mask. [In the *American Bibliopolist* for February, 1875.] New York: 1875.

TIMMINS, SAMUEL: The Lumley Portrait. [In *The American Bibliopolist* for June, 1875.] New York: 1875.

COSENS, F. W.: The Felton Portrait. [In *The American Bibliopolist* for August, 1875.] New York: 1875.

PAGE, WILLIAM: A Study of Shakespeare's Portraits. [In *Scribner's Monthly* for September, 1875.] New York: 1875.

NORRIS, J. PARKER: Page's Bust. [In *The American Bibliopolist* for October, 1875.] New York: 1875.

SCHAAFFHAUSEN, HERMANN: Ueber die Todtenmaske Shakespeare's. [In *Jahrbuch der Deutschen Shakespeare-Gesellschaft* for 1875.] 8vo. Weimar: 1875.

INGLEBY, C. M.: The Portraiture of Shakespeare. [Ten copies of Chapter V, of Dr. C. M. Ingleby's *Shakespeare: the Man, and the Book* were struck off, for private circulation, before the publication of that work, under the above title. It is slightly different from the same chapter in that book.] 4to. London: 1876.

NORRIS, J. PARKER: Opening Shakespeare's Grave. [In *American Bibliopolist* for April, 1876. The first proposal to open Shakespeare's grave.] 8vo. New York: 1876.

NORRIS, J. PARKER: Opening Shakespeare's Grave. [In *The Press* for August 4, 1876. A reprint of the proposal to open Shakespeare's grave, from *American Bibliopolist* for April, 1876.] Philadelphia: 1876.

ANONYMOUS: Shakespeare's *Carte de Visite*. [In *The Daily Mail* for August 23, 1876.] Birmingham: 1876.

ANONYMOUS: Opening of Shakespeare's Grave. [In *Daily Telegraph* for August 24, 1876.] London: 1876.

PAGE, WILLIAM: A Study of Shakespeare's Portraits. [Privately reprinted from Mr. Page's paper in *Scribner's Monthly* for September, 1875.] 32mo. London: 1876.

WINSOR, JUSTIN: A Bibliography of the Original Quartos and Folios of Shakespeare, etc. [Two hundred and fifty copies printed.] Folio. Boston: 1876.

PAGE, WILLIAM: A Study of Shakespeare's Portraits. [Reprinted from Mr. Page's paper in *Scribner's Monthly* for September, 1875.] 8vo. New York: 1877.

INGLEBY, C. M.: Shakespeare: the Man, and the Book. 4to. London: 1877.

ANONYMOUS: Opening of Shakespeare's Grave. [In *The Nation* for May 21, 1878.] New York: 1878.

NORRIS, J. PARKER: A Bibliography of Works on the Portraits of Shakespeare. [Privately printed.] 8vo. Philadelphia: 1879.

GOWER, RONALD: The Shakespeare Death Mask. [In *The Antiquary* for August, 1880.] London: 1880.

INGLEBY, C. M.: The Kesselstadt Miniature. [In *The Antiquary* for September, 1880.] London: 1880.

ANONYMOUS: Excavations in the Church and Churchyard of Stratford-upon-Avon. [In *Birmingham Daily Gazette* for December 17, 1880.] Birmingham: 1880.

HALLIWELL–PHILLIPPS, J. O.: Outlines of the Life of Shakespeare. 8vo. Brighton: 1881.

HALLIWELL–PHILLIPPS, J. O.: Outlines of the Life of Shakespeare. Second Edition. 8vo. London: 1882.

HALLIWELL–PHILLIPPS, J. O.: Outlines of the Life of Shakespeare. Third Edition. 8vo. London: 1883.

INGLEBY, C. M.: Shakespeare's Bones. 4to. London: 1883.

[TIMMINS, SAMUEL:] Shakespeare's Bones. [A Review of Dr. Ingleby's work entitled *Shakespeare's Bones*. In *Birmingham Daily Post* for August 15, 1883.] Birmingham: 1883.

ANONYMOUS: Shakespeare's Bones. [In *The Daily Mail* for August 16, 1883.] Birmingham: 1883.

ANONYMOUS: Shakespeare's Bones. [In *The Stratford-upon-Avon Herald* for August 17, 1883. Stratford-upon-Avon: 1883.

ANONYMOUS: Opening Shakespeare's Grave. [In *The Daily Telegraph* for September 3, 1883.] London: 1883.

ANONYMOUS: Opening Shakespeare's Grave. [In *The Standard* for September 3, 1883.] London: 1883.

ANONYMOUS: Opening Shakespeare's Grave. [In *The Morning Post* for September 3, 1883.] London: 1883.

ANONYMOUS: The Proposed Disinterment of Shakespeare's Remains. [In *The Daily Mail* for September 4, 1883.] Birmingham: 1883.

ANONYMOUS: The Proposed Vandalism at Shakespeare's Grave. [In *Birmingham Daily Gazette* for September 4, 1883.] Birmingham: 1883.

ANONYMOUS: The Proposal to Open Shakespeare's Tomb. [In *Birmingham Daily Gazette* for September 5, 1883.] Birmingham: 1883.

ANONYMOUS: The Proposed Exhumation of Shakespeare's Remains. [In *The Stratford-upon-Avon Herald* for September 7, 1883.] Stratford-upon-Avon: 1883.

ANONYMOUS: The Proposed Opening of Shakespeare's Tomb. [In *Birmingham Weekly Post* for September 8, 1883.] Birmingham: 1883.

SALA, GEORGE AUGUSTUS: Shakespeare's Bones. [In *Illustrated London News* for September 8, 1883.] London: 1883.

[BETTY, EDWARD:] Shakespeare's Skull. [In *Commercial Gazette* for September 23, 1883.] Cincinnati: 1883.

[BETTY, EDWARD:] Mortal Remains of Shakespeare. [In *Commercial Gazette* for October, 1883.] Cincinnati: 1883.

NORRIS, J. PARKER: The Portraits of Shakespeare. [In *Shakespeariana* from November, 1883, to September, 1884, both inclusive.] New York and Philadelphia: 1883–84.

RABONE, JOHN: Some Portraits of Shakespeare. [In the *Birmingham Daily Gazette* for November 20, 1883.] Birmingham: 1883.

LEIGHTON, WILLIAM: Review of *Shakespeare's Bones*. [In *Shakespeariana* for December, 1883.] New York: 1883.

NORRIS, J. PARKER: The Death Mask of Shakespeare. [Privately reprinted from *Shakespeariana* for February, 1884.] 8vo. Philadelphia: 1884.

[JONES, CHARLES:] How Shakespeare's Skull was Stolen and Found. 16mo. London: 1884.

RABONE, JOHN: A Lecture on Some Portraits of Shakespeare, etc. [Privately printed.] 8vo. Birmingham: 1884.

NORRIS, J. PARKER: Shall we open Shakespeare's Grave? [In *The Manhattan* for July, 1884.] New York: 1884.

KING, THOMAS D.: Shall we open Shakespeare's Grave? No. A Reply to the question put by Mr. J. Parker Norris in the July number of *The Manhattan*. [Privately printed.] 8vo. Montreal: 1884.

MORGAN, APPLETON: William Shakespeare's Grave. [In *Shakespeariana* for October, 1884.] Philadelphia: 1884.

[HALLIWELL-PHILLIPPS, J. O.:] Hand List of Drawings and Engravings illustrative of the Life of Shakespeare, etc. [Privately printed.] 8vo. Brighton: 1884.

HALLIWELL-PHILLIPPS, J. O.: Outlines of the Life of Shakespeare. Fourth Edition. Royal 8vo. London: 1884.

LEE, SIDNEY L.: Stratford-on-Avon from the Earliest Times to the Death of William Shakespeare. Folio. London: 1885.

SHALL WE OPEN SHAKESPEARE'S GRAVE? A PLEA FOR ASCERTAINING THE TRUE LIKENESS OF THE POET.

NINE years ago the present writer suggested the advisability of opening Shakespeare's grave and reverently examining his remains. Immediately after the publication of the suggestion a storm of abuse arose, during which the real merits of the proposal were lost sight of, and each critic vied with his brother in heaping opprobrious epithets on the head of him who had dared to suggest that which appeared to them to be a desecration of the poet's tomb.

"What do you expect to find but dust in the grave of one who has been buried over two hundred and fifty years?" was jeeringly asked by some of the critics.

But some of the seed that was then sown fell on good ground, and the idea has taken root in the minds of many. What may be the ultimate result it is difficult to say, but it is to be hoped that the advancement of scientific accuracy may yet conquer mere sentiment.

Lately Dr. C. M. Ingleby, Vice-President of the Royal Society of Literature, Honorary Member of the German Shakespeare Society, and Life Trustee of Shakespeare's Birthplace, Museum, and New Place, at Stratford-upon-Avon, has written an excellent little volume,* in which the proposal to open Shakespeare's grave is ably considered and a favorable conclusion arrived at.

It is the purpose of the present essay to discuss the question in all the aspects which have yet been presented, and to answer those persons who object to such an examination.

And first, as to the probability of finding anything but dust in the grave, much can be said. Shakespeare was buried underneath the chancel of the Church of Holy Trinity, at Stratford-upon-Avon, alongside of the graves of his wife, his daughter Susanna Hall, John Hall, her husband, and Thomas Nashe, the husband of Elizabeth, daughter of John and Susanna Hall. These graves lie side by side, and stretch across the chancel of the church, immediately in front of the rail separating the altar from the remainder of the chancel.

The situation of these graves shows that Shakespeare

---

* *Shakespeare's Bones*, etc. London: 1883. 4to.

and his family were persons of importance in the town of Stratford-upon-Avon, and make it very probable that the poet was buried in an hermetically-sealed leaden coffin. They were commonly used in those days for those whose relatives could afford them. If this conjecture be true, the remains will certainly be found in a much better state of preservation than if a wooden coffin alone was employed, although, even in the latter case, we must not despair of finding much that would be of the utmost value in determining his personal appearance.

Not many years ago some graves of those who were buried about the same time as Shakespeare were opened at Church Lawford, in England, and the faces, figures and even the very dresses of their occupants were quite perfect; but half an hour after the admission of air they became heaps of dust. A long enough period elapsed, however, to have enabled a photographer to have made successful pictures of them had any such preparations been thought of.

Very often the features and clothing of the dead are preserved for hundreds of years after burial, and, on opening their graves, wonderful sights have been seen. In a few minutes the remains often crumble away, and nothing but dust is left, but for a short time (long enough to take a photograph) the illusion is startling.

Think of a photograph of Shakespeare, "in his habit as he lived!" Would not such a relic be of inestimable value to the world, and what would not be given for such a treasure?

History furnishes us with many cases where the tombs of kings and queens have been opened, and their bodies, after the lapse of hundreds of years, appeared quite perfect.

In 1542 the Bishop of Bayeux obtained permission to examine the tomb of William the Conqueror. It will be remembered that he died in 1087, so that he had then lain in the grave four hundred and fifty-five years. When the stone covering the tomb was removed the body appeared entire, and in such a good state of preservation that the bishop had a painting made of the great king, as he lay there, by an artist of Caen. This he had hung up in the abbey, opposite to the tomb. The grave was then closed and remained untouched until 1562, when it was again opened, this time by irreverent hands. The Calvinists, under the command of Chastillon, had taken Caen, and opened the tomb under the idea that something of value would be found therein. The flesh had now disappeared from the bones, and nothing remained except the skeleton, wrapped in its clothes. These were thrown about the church and other indignities offered the bones.

Mary, a daughter of King Edward IV., a girl of fifteen, died in 1482, and was buried in St. George's Chapel, Windsor. In 1817, three hundred and thirty-five years after her burial, her tomb was opened. A curl of hair protruded from the coffin; and, on opening the latter, the girl's eyes, which were seen to be of a bright blue, were found to be open, and the face and figure quite perfect. On being exposed to the air the whole soon became dust, but the hair remained, and some of it was preserved by those who were present.

In 1789 the vault where her father was buried was also examined. He had likewise been interred in the Chapel of St. George, at Windsor. A leaden coffin surrounded the inner one of wood, and in the latter the skeleton of King Edward IV. was entire and perfect. The clothes in which he had been buried were probably removed by some one who had previously opened the tomb, for no trace of them was found. The hair was perfect and entire, and it was perhaps owing to this previous opening of the tomb, and the consequent admission of air, that the remains were not found in a still more perfect state. As King Edward IV. died in 1483, it consequently follows that an interval of three hundred and six years elapsed between the year of his burial and 1789, when the skeleton was found entire.

In 1813, during the search that was made in the vaults of St. George's Chapel by order of King George IV. for the body of King Charles I., Sir Henry Halford examined the remains of King Henry VIII., and commented on the very large frame of that much-married sovereign; and yet this was two hundred and sixty-six years after the king's death, which occurred in 1547.

Perhaps one of the most remarkable instances of finding the body of one who has long lain in the grave in a good state of preservation, is that of Katharine Parr, the sixth queen of King Henry VIII. She died in 1548, and was originally buried on the north side of the altar of the chapel of Sudley. In 1782, two hundred and thirty-four years after her entombment, the grave was opened. The leaden coffin having been cut open, the body was found carefully wrapped in a waxed cloth. This was removed, and it was discovered that the face was almost as it must have been when she was buried. The eyes of the dead queen were perfect. The inscription on the coffin showed that there could be no doubt as to the identity of the body. The earth was replaced in the grave, without the waxed cloth being placed over the face, and the leaden coffin was left open. Later in the summer of the same year a Mr. John Lucas again examined the body. He took off all the waxed cloth and found the entire body in a good state of preservation, notwithstanding the great time it had lain in the ground. The flesh of the arms was white and moist. Again the coffin was opened in 1784, and the body was this time taken out and rudely treated. Now the air had begun to do its work, and decay commenced. The body was again interred, but in October, 1786, a scientific examination of the remains was made by the Rev. Tredway Nash, F.A.S., who made a report of the result of his inquiries, which was published in Volume IX, of *Archæologia*, for 1787, being the Transactions of the Society of Antiquaries. Mr. Nash gives a *fac-simile* of the inscription on the leaden coffin, setting out the name of the deceased, her rank as queen to King Henry VIII., and her subsequent marriage to Thomas, Lord Sudley, and the date of her death. Mr. Nash further states that he then found the face decayed, and the teeth fallen. The body was perfect, the hands and nails of a brownish color. The covering in which the body had been wrapped, and which conduced to its former perfect preservation, until it was destroyed, consisted of linen, dipped in wax, tar and gums, and the external lead-covering followed the shape of the figure.

When King Charles I. was buried the coffin contained no inscription to designate its royal occupant, until one of his admirers supplied this want by wrapping around it a band of sheet lead, out of which had been cut spaces with a penknife, so that these formed large letters, which read, "CHARLES REX, 1649." Later, the very place where his coffin was deposited had been forgotten, until in 1813, on the occasion of the funeral of the Duchess of Brunswick, King George IV., attended by Sir Henry Halford and a number of noblemen, found it in a vault near the bodies of King Henry VIII. and his queen, Jane Seymour. Sir Henry has published an account of the opening of King Charles's coffin. He states that on April 1, 1813, the leaden coffin containing the remains was opened. Inside was found a wooden one, and on opening this the body was disclosed, wrapped in waxed cloths, covered with grease and resin. When these cloths were removed from the face, an impression of the dead king's features was plainly visible in them, and had plaster of Paris been poured into this mould, a cast of the face of the deceased could easily have been made. Sir Henry continues: "The complexion of the skin was dark and discolored. The forehead and temples had lost little or nothing of their muscular substance; the cartilage of the nose was gone; but the left eye, in the first moment of exposure, was open and full, though it vanished almost immediately; and the pointed beard, so characteristic of the reign of King Charles, was perfect. The shape of the face was a long oval; many of the teeth remained; and the left ear, in consequence of the interposition of the unctuous matter between it and the cerecloth, was found entire."

The head was loose, and was held up to view, as it had originally been, after having been severed from the unfortunate king's body. After a sketch had been made, and the identity of the body established beyond dispute, the head was returned to the coffin, the latter soldered up again, and replaced in the vault. At this time the skeleton of King Henry VIII., showing the beard on the chin, was also seen.

These instances of the opening of the graves of celebrated historical personages could easily be added to, but enough have been given above to show that bodies often remain far longer than Shakespeare's has done, and yet show a remarkable state of preservation.

Now, let us see if public sentiment has prevented the examination of the graves of those who were great in the walks of literature and art.

Schiller died May 9, 1805, at Weimar. Two days after his death the funeral took place, and his body was deposited in a vault which contained many coffins. In 1826 the vault was visited, Schiller's remains were removed, and, finally, in 1827, they were laid in a sarcophagus which had been built by direction of Goethe. Before they were finally entombed in this sarcophagus the bones and skull were carefully examined.

Raphael died April 6, 1520. In 1833 there was much dispute as to whether a skull which had been preserved in the Academy of St. Luke, at Rome, and claimed to be that of the great artist, was really his. On September 14, of the same year, the real remains of Raphael were found in a vault behind the high altar, in the Church of the Rotunda, and proven beyond a doubt to be his. A cast was made of the skull, and one from the right hand; and on October 18, 1833, the remains were re-interred in their former resting-place in a marble sarcophagus presented by Pope Gregory XVI.

Milton died November 8, 1674, and was buried four days afterward in St. Giles's Church, Cripplegate, London. His tomb was near the chancel. On August 4, 1790, a coffin was removed, and the supposed remains of the poet examined. It was discovered, however, that the bones which the coffin contained were those of a woman. Milton's remains are thought to still rest where they were originally deposited, but no feeling against their removal, and only the blundering of those who had the matter in charge, prevented their examination.

Burns died July 21, 1796, and in March, 1834, when

his tomb was opened to receive his wife's body, the poet's coffin was opened, and a cast of his head was made. Mr. Archibald Blacklock, a surgeon who was present, tells us that the cast was successfully made, as the bones of the skull were perfect, except "a little erosion of their external table," and were "firmly held together by their sutures," etc. The skull was then enclosed in a leaden case and buried where it was originally found.

Ben Jonson died August 6, 1637, and was buried in Westminster Abbey. His grave is directly under a square marble slab, inscribed "O RARE BEN JONSON;" and the tradition is that the poet was buried in a standing position. Frank Buckland, the well-known writer on natural history, took occasion to examine his tomb, when Sir Robert Wilson's grave was being made ready in its immediate vicinity. He says the workmen "found a coffin very much decayed, which, from the appearance of the remains, must have originally been placed in an upright position." A skull was found, which Buckland supposed was Ben Jonson's, and was removed by him. After examining it carefully he returned it to its original position. In 1859, when John Hunter's body was brought to the Abbey, the same place was again exposed. Again Mr. Buckland secured what he supposed was the poet's skull, and after making a further examination of it, returned it to its resting-place. Shortly after this a communication appeared in the London *Times* to the effect that "the skull of Ben Jonson was in the possession of a blind gentleman at Stratford-upon-Avon." Hereupon Mr. Buckland made further inquiries, and tells us that "he has convinced himself that the skull which he had taken such care of on two occasions was not Ben Jonson's skull at all; that a Mr. Ryde had anticipated him both times in removing and replacing the genuine article, and that the Warwickshire claimant was a third skull which Mr. Ryde observed had been purloined from the grave on the second opening."

Mr. Buckland was satisfied that Mr. Ryde's skull was the genuine one, because he (Mr. Ryde) described his skull as having red hair. No authority exists for supposing that Ben had this colored hair, but the poet himself says that his hair was black, and a portrait of him so represents him. Jonson was sixty-five when he died, and had his hair been originally either red or black, as Lieutenant-Colonel Cunningham observes (in his edition of Gifford's Ben Jonson), it would not then have been any other color than gray.

Sir Francis Bacon, one of the greatest and yet also the least of men (for his life shows a wonderful fall from high position), he whom a class of seekers after notoriety, in the shape of a new sensation, would claim as the author of the immortal Shakespeare's works, died in 1626. He was buried in St. Michael's Church, St. Albans. On the occasion of the burial of the last Lord Verulam, a search was made for the remains of Sir Francis, during which a partition wall of the vault was pulled down, and the ground under his monument was explored, but they could not be found.

Suppose, for the sake of argument, that on opening Shakespeare's grave we should find nothing but his skull and a few bones. Of what good would they be to us? This question has been well answered by Dr. Ingleby in the work above cited. He says that "beyond question, the skull of Shakespeare, might we discover it in anything like its condition at the time of its interment, would be of still greater interest and value than Schiller's or Raphael's. It would at least settle two disputed points in the Stratford bust; it would test the Droeshout print, and every one of the half-dozen portraits-in-oil which pass as presentments of Shakespeare's face at different periods of his life. Moreover, it would pronounce decisively on the pretensions of the Kesselstadt Death Mask, and we should know whether that was from the 'flying mould' after which Gerard Johnson worked when he sculptured the bust. Negative evidence the skull would assuredly furnish; but there is reason for believing that it would afford positive evidence in favor of the bust, one or other of the portraits, or even of the Death Mask; and why, I ask, should not an attempt be made to recover Shakespeare's skull?"

After reading the above passage from Dr. Ingleby's book, Dr. J. O. Halliwell-Phillipps wrote to the Mayor and Corporation of Stratford-upon-Avon, protesting against any opening of the poet's grave. He said that even if a skull were found in the grave its evidence would not weigh against that of the bust, for, he added, if its formation did not correspond with that of the effigy "the inference would naturally be that it was not Shakespeare's." Whose skull would it be if not the poet's? Does Dr. Halliwell-Phillipps think that any one has already opened the grave, taken away the real skull, and substituted another? There is no record of anyone else having been buried in the same grave as Shakespeare. The graves of his wife and family are side by side, near his, as has already been stated; and there was no one else at all likely to have been interred with him in the same grave.

Within the last few months a Mr. James Hare, of Birmingham, wrote to a local paper of that town, giving a remarkable account of a visit to Shakespeare's grave.

Mr. Hare said that either in 1826 or 1827 he went to Stratford-upon-Avon with a friend, and on visiting the poet's tomb they found the vault adjoining it was open, as he thinks, for an addition to its contents; that he and his friend got into the adjoining vault, and stood upon a board. While there they looked through an opening in the wall that separated Shakespeare's tomb from the one they were standing in, and that he could see nothing in it but "a slight elevation of mouldering dust on its level floor, and the smallness of the quantity surprised me. No trace or appearance of a coffin or undecomposed bones, and certainly no such elevation as a skull, for instance, would occasion; and the impression produced by its then present state was that the remains were enclosed in an ordinary wooden coffin, and simply laid on the floor of the vault, be that floor what it may. If a leaden casket had been used it would have been present in some form or other, or had an amount of earth been dug out to bury it below the surface, a depression would have been the natural consequence of the decay beneath, and the elevation could not then be accounted for."

No doubt Mr. Hare gives a truthful account of what he saw, or thought he saw, but the question is, could he reasonably expect to see anything under the circumstances? He was standing in a vault, looking through an opening into an adjoining one that was, of course, very dimly lighted by the crevice—if, indeed, it was not all dark, as it probably was. In such darkness, with his eyes not accustomed to the gloom, what could he see? If there had been a leaden coffin in which the poet was buried, it would, in all probability, have enclosed a wooden one in which the body rested. This would have made the leaden one very large, and it would probably have occupied the whole of the floor of the vault, which was only made for one coffin, and could easily have been mistaken by Mr. Hare for the bottom of the vault. The "slight elevation of mouldering dust" that he speaks of, was probably some of the cement or mortar that had fallen from the sides of the vault.

Another thing must be here noted, and that is, that there was a regularly built vault in which the poet was buried, and not an ordinary grave dug in the earth. Such a vault, with stone or brick sides, would be much more conducive to the preservation of a body than the mere earth. But the leaden coffin, in which the poet was in all probability buried, would render the remains impervious to all damp, and "water is a sore decayer of your whoreson dead body," as the grave-digger in *Hamlet* well remarks.

Much has been written, by those of a sentimental turn of mind, about the doggerel lines cut on the stone which covers the poet's grave; and they have even been called "the touching epitaph, written by the poet himself, imploring that his remains should be allowed to rest in peace."

There is not the slightest evidence to warrant the belief that they were written by Shakespeare, and the evidence of the lines themselves is strong presumptive proof against such a belief.

No one who has carefully read and studied the poet's works can really believe that he wrote such lame and halting verses as these:

> "Good frend for Iesus sake forbeare,
> To digg the dvst encloased heare:
> Bleste be ye man yt spares thes stones,
> And cvrst be he yt moves my bones."

They were probably placed over the grave by some member of his family, to prevent the removal of his body to the old charnel-house which formerly adjoined the chancel of the church. Shakespeare may have seen this, with the neglected piles of bones that filled it, and have conceived the idea, which he afterward expressed to his family, that he would not have wished his remains to be placed where there was such confusion and neglect. This charnel-house was taken down in 1800.

Had we a likeness of the poet, executed by a competent artist, and of undoubted authority, there would perhaps be no occasion to examine Shakespeare's remains. But here we are all at sea. Only two "counterfeit presentments" of the poet have a well proven pedigree—the bust in the chancel of the Church of Holy Trinity, Stratford-upon-Avon, and the print published in the First Folio edition of the plays. The former was the work of one whose occupation it was to sculpture the rude effigies of the dead which were placed on their monuments—for of such ability were Gerard Johnson and his sons, and nothing more. No one has ever pretended to claim for the sculptor any artistic merit. The figure is rudely cut out of a block of soft stone, and though some have seen fit to praise it, none can look upon its manifest defects without wishing to know if he who wrote for all time did really inhabit such a body as this.

As for the print of Martin Droeshout, published in the First Folio, it is even worse than the bust. It has no claim to rank as a work of art, it is not known from what it is copied, and many think it unlike any human being.

Now comes the trouble. Both of these representations of Shakespeare are well authenticated, and they are the only ones that are, but are they like one another? *No*, they are not. Many have thought they saw a certain resemblance between them, but the wish to do so was the father of the thought. They are very different. Which is the correct one, or is either a true likeness? The bust was probably erected by his family, and may reasonably be supposed to have some resemblance to him; while the engraving is certified to be a correct likeness by his friend Ben Jonson.

All the other portraits, and there are more than a dozen, are doubtful, to say the least. The famous Chandos Portrait, which is the commonly accepted likeness of the poet, has a very doubtful pedigree. The Death Mask represents a noble face, and one which all would wish that Shakespeare really did resemble, but its pedigree is very defective, and only a certain likeness can be traced in it to the authenticated portraits.

Shakespeare's skull would set all these doubts at rest, even if we found nothing more in the grave. But if, by good fortune, a photograph of the poet's face could be made, would not the end justify the means taken to secure it? That such a hope is not a wild impossibility is known to science, and the instances given above of the opening of the graves of many poets and others, would seem to lead to but one conclusion, that the world will not rest satisfied until the experiment has been tried, and the tomb at Stratford-upon-Avon made to give up its mystery. Let it be done reverently, but let it be done soon. Every year that rolls by of course helps to defeat the end that is to be attained. But that it will finally be done is surely but a question of time.

# The Stratford Bust.

PHOTOGRAPH OF ORIGINAL BY TH

THE STRATFORD BUST.

THE Stratford Bust is the oldest, and probably the best authenticated of all the representations of Shakespeare which have come down to us. It is erected on the inside wall, on the north side of the chancel of Holy Trinity Church, at Stratford-upon-Avon, at a distance of about five feet from the floor. Underneath the floor of the chancel, in front of the monument, are the graves of Shakespeare and his family.

It was sculptured either by Gerard Johnson or one of his sons. Johnson was a native of Amsterdam, who afterwards came to London to follow his business of sculptor and "tombe-maker." In 1593 he had been in England for twenty-six years, and it is quite probable, therefore, that in 1616, when Shakespeare died, Gerard Johnson was too old to work himself and allowed one of his sons to make this monument.

Gerard Johnson resided in St. Thomas Apostle's, in the Ward of Vintry, London, and had five sons, four journeymen, two apprentices and "one Englishman." He appears to have done quite an extensive business in "tombe-making," as his trade was then called.

Dugdale speaks in his Diary, 1653, (which was published in 1827,*) of "Shakespeares and John Combes monuments, at Stratford super Avon, made by one Gerard Johnson."

John Combe left £60 for the erection of his tomb, which he directed by his will, should be finished within a year from the date of his death. Combe died in 1614, but his will was proved in November, 1615, and his executors probably did not set about its erection until the following Spring, when Shakespeare died. The family of the latter may have chosen the same time to order the monument to the poet's memory, as they are both by the same sculptor.

The exact date of the erection of the monument and bust is not known, however, but it was probably shortly after Shakespeare's death, in 1616. When the First Folio edition of his works was published, in 1623, it contained these lines:

---

* *Life, Diary,* etc. 4to. 1827, p. 99.

TO THE MEMORIE

of the deceased Authour Maister

W. Shakespeare.

Shake-speare, *at length thy pious fellowes giue*
The world thy Workes: thy Workes, by which, out-liue
Thy Tombe, thy name must: when that stone is rent,
And Time dissolues thy Stratford *Moniment,*
Here we aliue shall view thee still.   This Booke,
When Brasse and Marble fade, shall make thee looke
Fresh to all Ages: when Posteritie
Shall loath what's new, thinke all is prodegie
That is not Shake-speares; *eu'ry Line, each Verse*
Here shall reuiue, redeeme thee from thy Herse.
Nor Fire, nor cankring Age, as Naso *said,*
Of his, thy wit-fraught Booke shall once inuade.
Nor shall I e're beleeue, or thinke thee dead
(Though mist) vntill our bankrout Stage be sped
(Impossible) with some new straine t' out-do
Passions of Iuliet, *and her* Romeo;
Or till I heare a Scene more nobly take,
Then when thy half-sword parlying Romans *spake.*
Till these, till any of thy Volumes rest
Shall with more fire, more feeling be exprest,
Be sure, our Shake-speare, *thou canst neuer dye,*
But crown'd with Lawrell, liue eternally.
L. Digges.

The words, "And Time dissolues thy Stratford Moniment," evidently refer to the present one; which has remained from the date of its erection to the present time.

The bust and the cushion in front of it are made of bluish limestone, which is quite soft. It is the size of life, and is rough on the back, and there is an indentation at the back of the head. The columns on each side are now of black marble, polished, while their capitals and bases are of freestone, gilded. The columns are of the Corinthian order of architecture.

All of the entablatures were formerly of white alabaster, but these were taken out in 1749, owing to their having decayed, and the marble ones were substituted.

Above the bust is an arch surmounting the niche in which it rests. Over this are the arms of Shakespeare, on either side of which are two cherubim, one of whom holds a spade, and the other an inverted torch, while he rests his hand on a skull. On the apex of the monument is another skull.

Underneath the cushion, in front of the bust, is the following inscription, on an oblong tablet:

IVDICIO PYLIVM, GENIO SOCRATEM, ARTE MARONEM
TERRA TEGIT, POPVLVS MÆRET, OLYMPVS HABET

THE STRATFORD BUST. 25

Stay Passenger why goest thov by so fast?
read if thov canst, whom enviovs Death hath plast,
with in this monvment Shakspeare: with whome,
qvick natvre dide: whose name, doth deck yᔆ Tombe,
far more, then cost: Sieh all, yᵗ He hath writt,
Leaves living art, bvt page, to serve his witt.

obiit ano do! 1616
Ætatis 53 die 23 ap.

This inscription was certainly not written by a native of Stratford, for it refers to the body of Shakespeare being "within this monument," when we know that his grave is under the floor of the chancel, in front of the monument.

Shakespeare is represented as composing his works. The right hand holds a pen while the left rests on a paper on the cushion. The effigy was originally painted in colors to resemble life. The face and hands were of a flesh color; the eyes of a light hazel; the hair and the beard were auburn. The doublet was scarlet, and the loose gown without sleeves worn over it, was black. The upper portion of the cushion was green, the lower red, with gilt tassels on the corners.

In 1749 the monument had become somewhat dilapidated, and in that year it was repaired. The money for this purpose was raised by a performance of *Othello*, which was given in the Town Hall, at Stratford-upon-Avon.

At this time (1749) the marble entablatures were substituted for the alabaster ones which had become decayed, and the colors were renewed, care being taken to preserve the original tints. A forefinger of the right hand and a portion of the thumb of the same, which were broken off, together with the pen which had been between the fingers, were also replaced at the same time. In 1790 it again became necessary to replace these pieces of stone, which were missing, and William Roberts of Oxford was selected to do the work.

In 1793 Edmond Malone (who had published an edition of the poet's works in 1790), advised the vicar of Holy Trinity Church to have the bust painted white. This was done, apparently by an ordinary house painter, whose coarse brush left lines in the paint. Malone's classical taste was offended by the coloring *ad vivum*, but apart from the vandalism of thus injuring so interesting and valuable a relic of the great poet, he seems to have forgotten that the Greeks frequently colored their statues.

This white paint was allowed to remain on the bust until 1861, when it was removed by Simon Collins, a restorer of pictures residing in London. Mr. Collins went to Stratford-upon-Avon, and on removing the white paint he found that enough of the old coloring remained to enable him to restore the bust to its original colors.

The Stratford Bust.

From Photograph of Original by Thrupp.

Speaking of this restoration, Mr. J. O. Halliwell-Phillipps says:

"This step was induced by the seriously adverse criticism to which the operation of 1793 had been subjected, but although the action then taken was undoubtedly injudicious, it did not altogether obliterate the semblance of an intellectual human being, and this is more than can be said of the miserable travesty which now distresses the eye of the pilgrim." *

Whether the bust looked better in its white state, or when colored, is a question as to which there has been much difference of opinion; but as it was originally colored it certainly was only proper that the colors should have been restored. Any one who has seen a cast from the bust in a white or gray state, would hardy know it for the same statue as the colored one, so much does the coloring alter the expression.

Mr. Halliwell-Phillipps writing of the bust before Malone's paint had been removed, said:

"The bust, when minutely examined, contains indications of individuality that render such a supposition" [*i. e.*, that it was a fanciful likeness] "altogether inadmissible; for no artist, working either from a picture, or rely-

---

* *Outlines of the Life of Shakespeare*, 4th edition. London: 1884, 8vo., p. 231.

ing on memory, description, or imagination, would have introduced the peculiarities which belong to it, amongst which may be specially noticed the slight but singular fall of the cheek under the right eye, which has been attributed to the sculptor copying from a cast taken after death. The forehead and the formation of the head should alone be decisive evidences in favor of its authenticity. There is, in truth, a convincing and a mental likeness in this monument, one that grows upon us by contemplation, and makes us unwilling to accept any other resemblance. If it has fallen beneath a cloud, the reason must be sought for in the circumstance that an image, the composition of which derives no assistance from the ideal, can scarcely be expected to satisfy the imagination in the delineation of features belonging to so great an intellect. But to those who can bring themselves to believe that, notwithstanding his unrivalled genius, Shakespeare was a realization of existence, and in his daily career, much as other men were, the bust at Stratford will convey very nearly all that it is desirable to know of his outward form." *

Friswell speaks of the bust in very unflattering terms: "The skull of the figure, rudely cut and heavy, with-

---

* *The Works of William Shakespeare.* London: 1853, folio, Vol. I, p. 230.

out any feeling, is a mere block; a phrenologist would be puzzled at its smoothness and roundness. It has no more individuality or power in it than a boy's marble. The cheeks are fat and sensual, the neck just rounded out of the soft stone; the linen collar of the dress like a sheet of bent block tin." *

Dr. C. M. Ingleby's opinion is also unfavorable:

"How awkward is the *ensemble* of the face! What a painful stare, with its goggle eyes and gaping mouth! The expression of this face has been credited with *humor*, *bonhommie*, *hilarity* and *jollity*. To me it is decidedly *clownish;* and it is suggestive of a man crunching a sour apple, or struck with amazement at some unpleasant spectacle. Yet there is force in the lineaments of this muscular face. One can hardly doubt that it is an unintentional caricature; but for that very reason it should be an unmistakeable likeness." †

Boaden thus refers to the head of the figure:

"The contour of the head is well given. The lips are very carefully carved; but the eyes appear to me to be of a very poor character: the curves of the lids have no grace—the eyes themselves no protecting prominences

---

* *Life Portraits of William Shakespeare.* London: 1864, 8vo., p. 10.
† *Shakespeare: the Man, and the Book.* Part I, p. 79. London: 1877, 4to.

of bone, and the whole of this important feature is tame and superficial." *

Wivell remarks that "the nose and forehead are fine; and were it not for a rather disproportionate length from the former to the mouth, the face would be remarkably handsome. It has a more fleshy appearance than any of the other portraits, and has much less of the look of a Jew than most of them, as his beard is trimmed to the fashion of the time." †

Some years ago William Page, a celebrated artist, made a study of the principal portraits of Shakespeare, for the purpose of making a bust of the poet. His views about the Stratford bust are particularly valuable. He says:

"The most inexpert observer may see, by placing a cast of it beside a fine antique or an excellent modern portrait, what I mean when I say that it shows very crude and unskilled modelling. This does not mean it may not have many individual characteristics. Artists and others have always known that the eyes were impossible, the nose worked off too short, or the end of it never reached, as the spot where it should join the

---

* *An Inquiry*, etc. London: 1824, 8vo., p. 31.
† *An Inquiry*, etc. London: 1827, 8vo., p. 140.

upper lip is still marked in the bust; and had the nose started out at right angles to the lip at that place, instead of slanting up to its present point, truth and beauty each would have been subserved. Though carelessly, falsely, and hence wickedly misinterpreted in many ways, still there are fixed facts in this bust which make it valuable in some points of likeness. * * * * * The left side is flattened away from the mouth back toward the middle of the cheek. This was probably a true characteristic of his" [*i. e.*, Gerard Johnson's] "model. Then the lower part of his cheek is fattened out and made very full under the jaw. This characteristic is probably exaggerated if it existed at all, the sculptor supposing that the flesh of the cheeks in the reclining posture fell back, and should be replaced in this manner, since he represented his subject upright. On the right side of the mouth there is a contrasting fullness of the cheek, and then a falling away diagonally to the jaw, from which, around to the throat, you find the line less curved than on the other side. The individual character of this one-sidedness, which exists in some way in every face, was doubtless founded on a mask from nature, and is exactly graded, recorded and interpreted in the German Mask. The Greeks valued these natural inequalities. The Venus of Milo's face is one-sided, and the Theseus's eyebrows unlike.

"I should have stated before, that when I speak of right and left side I mean Shakespeare's, and not the observer's.

"In the Stratford bust the lower lip is peculiar, the right side being sensibly fuller and hanging down lower than the left side. It is crudely rendered, yet a fact safely lodged there can never be ousted. There is also an indentation at the left corner of the mouth, more accentuated than on the other side, which is dragged down rather vertically toward the chin.

"The sculptor certainly had some guide for these varieties of undulations. The luckiest guess does not hit in a portrait. These personal peculiarities exist in the Mask, where they are seen not to have been exaggerated by death."*

F. W. Fairholt, F.S.A., made a very careful drawing of the bust for Halliwell-Phillipps' Folio Edition of Shakespeare, and was much impressed by the excellence with which the monument was executed. He believed the face to have been sculptured with singular delicacy and care except the eyes.

---

* *A Study of Shakespeare's Portraits.* London: 1876, 24mo., p. 16.

Many persons have thought that the face of the effigy was made after a mask taken from life, or from a dead face. John Bell, a distinguished sculptor, believed this, and Sir Francis Chantrey, another sculptor of eminence, is said to have shared in this opinion also.

If this be true it would account for the poorness of the eyes, which are mere elliptical openings. The cast (if the sculptor worked from one) would show the eyes closed, and his skill not being sufficient to enable him to successfully represent them open, would account for his failure in this respect.

If the cast were taken after death the cheeks would probably have presented a somewhat sunken appearance; and in the effort to restore this deficiency, the sculptor might easily have made the cheeks too full, as they now appear to be.

The shortness of the nose, and the unusual length of the upper lip, have been frequently noticed and commented upon. In 1814 John Britton was the means of inducing George Bullock to make a cast of the effigy. The vicar of the church (who was then the Rev. Dr. Davenport), and the parochial authorities, having given permission, the bust was taken down from the niche in which it rests, and a successful mould made from it. Britton states that Bullock found it "in a decayed and dangerous state" and further that "it would be risking its destruction to remove it again."*

R. B. Wheler, the well known antiquarian of Stratford-upon-Avon, and author of one of the best local histories of that town, was present when Bullock took the bust down from its niche, and stated, in a letter to Britton, that there was no date or inscription on the back of the effigy.†

When Bullock had finished making his mould of the bust, he made a cast from it, and invited Sir Walter Scott, Benjamin West, Dr. Spurzheim, and John Britton, to breakfast with him. It was on this occasion that Bullock made a cast of Scott's head.

These gentlemen entered into a discussion about the cast of the Stratford bust, which was in the room. Dr. Spurzheim and Benjamin West both commented upon the characteristics of the bust, and the latter on this occasion said that the eyes, nose, mouth, forehead, cheeks and hair were all "imitations of nature, modelled from the person whilst living, or from a cast after death. There was no appearance of fancy, or of its having been modelled merely from recollection."‡

---

* *Appendix to Britton's Auto-Biography.* London: 1850, 8vo., p. 6.
† *Ibid*, p. 13.
‡ *Ibid*, p. 8.

Sir Walter Scott particularly commented on the great space between the nose and the upper lip, and all the others agreed with him that the sculptor must have made an error here. Bullock declared that Scott had the same peculiarity to an even greater degree than Shakespeare, as shown in the bust. A pair of compasses were produced, and Scott's upper lip was found to be a quarter of an inch further from his nose than Shakespeare's.*

There was originally a stone pen in the right hand of the effigy, but it is related that a young man who had taken it out of the fingers to examine it, dropped it on the floor of the chancel, where it was broken to pieces. A quill pen dipped in ink now replaces it.

To most people the bust is at first sight disappointing —especially if seen in its colored state. It grows upon one, however, the more it is looked at, and a white or gray cast from it becomes very pleasing after long familiarity with it.

It certainly was erected shortly after Shakespeare's death, and probably by some of his family. It was put in a conspicuous place in the chancel of his native church, and in the sight of his fellow townsmen. Even if we admit that its sculptor was nothing more than a "tombe-

---

* *Appendix to Britton's Auto-Biography.* London: 1850, 8vo., p. 8.

maker," as he undoubtedly was, still the bust must have had strong points of resemblance to the poet or it would not have been accepted. Rudely cut it certainly is, and it possesses no claims to being a work of art.

Its appearance is very different when viewed from different positions. Looked at from underneath the very full appearance of the cheeks and the throat is especially noticeable. Seen from a level the effect is much better, while a three-quarters view is the most pleasing. The nose is undoubtedly very short, and the supposition that it met with an accident while the sculptor was working at it would not seem altogether improbable, if we did not remember that other faces have been met with in life with the same peculiarity—notably that of Sir Walter Scott, already referred to.

A large number of engravings have been executed which pretend to represent the bust, but the majority of them utterly fail to do so.

Rowe's edition of Shakespeare, London: 1709, 16mo. (Vol. I, p. xxxvii,), contains an engraving of the monument and bust which is almost a caricature. The cherubim are represented as balancing themselves over the top, with their legs hanging down; the one who should have the inverted torch is holding an hour glass, and the other holds up the spade instead of leaning on it. The

The Stratford Bust.

From Photograph of Original.

head of the bust looks more like the Chandos portrait than the bust, while Shakespeare is represented as patting a pillow with both hands instead of resting his hands on the cushion, as in the original. Only two lines of the inscription underneath are given.

An engraving by G. Vertue, published in Pope's edition of Shakespeare, London: 1725, 4to., gives the monument (Vol. I, p. xxxi,) with tolerable accuracy, except that one of the cherubim is represented with a candle instead of the spade which he really holds in his hand, and the other hand rests on an hour glass instead of a rock; while the other cherub is seated on the skull, instead of resting his hand on it. The torch in his hand is upright also, instead of inverted, as it should be. The bust, however, as represented in this picture has the head taken from the Chandos portrait. It is a striking illustration of the inaccuracy of some of the older engravers.

H. Gravelot has evidently copied Vertue's plate for Hanmer's edition of Shakespeare, London: 1744, 4to. (Vol. I, p. xxxiii,), as that plate is almost an exact copy of it, except that the hair is not as well engraved. The Chandos head appears on the bust in this plate also. This same plate of Gravelot's was used in Hanmer's second edition of Shakespeare, London: 1771, 4to. (Vol. I, p. xxii.)

Grignion engraved a poor copy of the plate which was published in Rowe's Shakespeare (1709) for Bell's edition of the poet's works, London: 1788, 24mo. (Vol. II, p. 468. The plate is dated 1786.)

A poor plate, drawn by S. Harding, and engraved by A. Birrell, was published in Harding's *Shakespeare Illustrated*, London: 1793.

Samuel Ireland published an engraving of the monument, from a drawing by himself, in his *Picturesque Views on the Upper, or Warwickshire Avon*, London: 1795, 8vo. The bust is represented so badly that it is a mere caricature.

The earliest engraving of the bust that did it anything like justice was published in Boydell's Folio Edition of Shakespeare, London: 1802, Vol. I. It is engraved by J. Neagle, from a drawing by J. Boydell. The monument is correctly represented, with the exception that the cherubim have torches, instead of only one. The figure of the bust is too short, the hand that holds the pen is badly drawn, and the face is less full than that of the original.

When Wheler's *History and Antiquities of Stratford-upon-Avon* was published in 1806, it contained an engraving of the monument by F. Eginton, from a drawing by Wheler. The monument is fairly well represented, but the bust has not fared so well. Wheler has elongated the face and changed its expression entirely.

A very handsome mezzotint, representing the bust alone, engraved by William Ward, and published by J. Britton, in 1816, is by far the best picture of the bust that had appeared at that time; and in a collection of prints it is sure to command attention by its admirable appearance. The head and figure are very well drawn, and the black background brings out the bust in striking relief.

W. T. Fry engraved a plate of the bust, from a cast by Bullock, which was published by Caddell and Davies, in Drake's *Shakespeare and his Times*, London: 1817, 4to. It is a three-quarter face view, and has great merit.

Robert Smirke, R.A., was an artist of some merit, but his picture of the bust, engraved by R. Ashby, and published by Hurst, Robinson & Co., *circa* 1820, certainly did not add to his reputation. It is entirely unlike the original.

All of the above mentioned engravings represented the bust in its white state, but the first one that showed it in colors was engraved by W. Finden, from a drawing by J. Thurston, and published by W. Walker, in 1820. The lower part of the jaw is very badly done, but otherwise the engraving is admirable. This same plate, very much worn, was afterwards used in Charles Cowden Clarke's *Shakespeare Characters*, London: 1863, 8vo.

A very poor copy of the bust only, in its white state, was engraved by Fry, and published by F. C. & J. Rivington, June 25, 1821, in Vol. III of Boswell's edition of Malone's Shakespeare, London: 1821, 8vo.

E. Scriven engraved a handsome plate of the head and shoulders of the bust, from a drawing by J. Boaden, published in Boaden's *Inquiry*, London: 1824, 8vo. It represents the bust as white, and the cheeks are too full, but the top of the head is very fine. Boaden must have stood below the bust when making his drawing, and hence this picture gives the head too flat an appearance. Had he been on a level with his subject, this defect would have been remedied.

Wivell drew a fine picture of the bust only, which was very well engraved in stipple by I. S. Agar, and published by George Lawford, in 1825. It shows the bust in its white state, and the view is almost directly in front. It is most creditable both to the artist and engraver, and will always be sought for as being among the best engravings of the bust that have been published.

Another drawing by Wivell, engraved by T. A. Dean, and published in Wivell's *Inquiry*, London: 1827, 8vo., is of the head and shoulders only, and is not as successful as the one above mentioned. It shows the bust in its white state.

In Wivell's *Inquiry*, London: 1827, 8vo., is also an engraving of the whole monument by W. Wallis, from a drawing in the possession of J. Britton. The effigy is by Wivell, however, and though small, is quite well done.

Valpy's Shakespeare, London: 1832, 16mo., Vol. I, p. xli, contains a poor engraving by Starling.

Illustrations of Stratford-upon-Avon, published by Ward, in 1851, folio, contains an interesting lithograph of the monument, showing the bust in its white state. It is well drawn and tolerably accurate, but the cheeks are not full enough.

A fair engraving of the bust by G. Greatbach, from a drawing by T. D. Scott, was published in Vol. II of Tallis' Shakespeare. (1851?)

A very accurately drawn and carefully engraved copy of the whole monument, by F. W. Fairholt, was published in Halliwell-Phillipps' Folio Shakespeare, Vol. I, London: 1853. Mr. Fairholt evidently has taken great pains with his work, but there is an expression about the face in his engraving which is different from the original.

Singer's second edition of Shakespeare, London: 1856, 16mo., Vol. I, contains an engraving of the bust only, by E. Radclyffe, which is fair.

A small engraving, (with no engraver's name,) appeared in Knight's Cabinet Shakespeare, London: 1856, 24mo., Vol. X; and another in Vol. XI of the same work.

Dyce's first edition of Shakespeare, London: 1857, 8vo., Vol. I, has a good engraving of the bust only, by Francis Holl. The same plate was used in Dyce's second edition of the poet's works, London: 1866, 8vo., Vol. I, and also in the third edition of the same work, London: 1875, 8vo., Vol. II.

Staunton's edition of Shakespeare, London: 1858, royal 8vo., contains a good engraving of the bust, drawn by E. W. Robinson, and engraved by H. Robinson. The same plate was used in Staunton's Library Edition, London: 1863, 8vo.

A fair engraving on wood of the bust, by W. J. Linton, was published in Wise's *Shakespeare, his Birth-place*, etc., London: 1861, 16mo.

No engraving, however good, is able to represent the bust as it really is, and it remains for the camera to give us a faithful copy of the effigy.

Small photographs of the monument were published in Hunter's *Shakespeare and Stratford*, London: 1864, 16mo., and in Jephson's *Shakespeare: his Birthplace*, etc., London: 1864, 8vo.; but the one in Friswell's *Life Portraits*, London: 1864, 8vo., is far better. It is undoubtedly the best small photograph of the monument that has been published, and gives a good idea of it. The photographs in different copies of the book vary somewhat, however, owing to their having been printed from several negatives, and some are not as good as others.

In 1864 John Burton & Sons published some large photographs of the monument, taken by Thrupp, of Birmingham, which cannot be excelled, and which admirably represent the monument as it is. The camera has evidently been placed on a level with the monument in taking the negatives, and the result is therefore highly satisfactory. Some of these photographs show the whole monument, and others, which are larger, give nearly all of it.

Bell's Shakespeare, London: 1865, 16mo., Vol. I, has a fair engraving of the bust, but the engraver's name is not given.

Two fine photographs of the bust, (but taken from a white cast,) showing a front and side view, accompany Gabriel Harrison's privately printed brochure, entitled *The Stratford Bust*, Brooklyn: 1865, 4to.

In Walter's *Shakespeare's Home and Rural Life*, London: 1874, folio, there was published a very good heliotype of the monument.

Numerous photographs have since been taken, all of which give a better idea of the bust than engravings do—unless the latter are made from them.

In 1882 the New Shakespeare Society published a large phototype of the monument, which would be all that could be desired, were it not for a certain blurred appearance that is noticeable in parts of it. It is taken from directly in front of the monument, and on a level with it.

The following year, 1883, the same Society issued a chromo-phototype of the monument, which gives the present colors of the effigy, the entablature, etc. It is well done, and is a valuable representation of this very interesting relic of the great poet.

The Droeshout Engraving.

From Photo-Lithograph of Original by Day and Son.

THE DROESHOUT ENGRAVING.

IN 1623 was published the first collected edition of Shakespeare's plays, generally known as the First Folio. It was edited by John Heminge and Henry Condell, Shakespeare's friends and fellow actors, and is of folio size. On the title-page, in a space left for the purpose, this engraving appears. The plate is about 7½ inches long by 6⅓ wide. Under the lower left hand corner of the latter is the inscription: "Martin Droeshout sculpsit London." The same plate was used in the Second (1632), Third (1663 and 1664), and Fourth (1685) Folio editions of Shakespeare. In the Second Folio the plate appeared in the same position as in the first edition, and this is also the case in the copies of the Third Folio that are dated 1663; but in copies of that edition dated 1664 the engraving is on a leaf opposite to, and facing the title-page, and surmounting the verses by

Ben Jonson referred to below. In the Fourth Folio the engraving occupies the same place that it does in copies of the third edition dated 1664.

In the first, second, and 1663 copies of the third edition, opposite the title-page, and facing it, on the back of the leaf which generally bears the bastard title in books, are printed the following verses by Ben Jonson:

To the Reader.

This Figure, that thou here seest put,
   It was for gentle Shakespeare cut;
Wherein the Grauer had a strife
   with Nature, to out-doo the life:
O, could he but have drawne his wit
   As well in brasse, as he hath hit
His face; the Print would then surpasse
   All, that vvas euer vvrit in brasse.
But, since he cannot, Reader, looke
   Not on his Picture, but his Booke.
                                        B. I.

In copies of the third edition dated 1664, and in the Fourth Folio, these verses, with some unimportant typographical variations, appear on the same page as the portrait and surmounted by it—that is, facing the title-page.

Title=Page of The First Folio.

SHOWING HOW THE DROESHOUT ENGRAVING APPEARED IN IT.

Mr. WILLIAM
SHAKESPEARES
COMEDIES,
HISTORIES, &
TRAGEDIES.

Publifhed according to the True Originall Copies.

LONDON
Printed by Ifaac Iaggard, and Ed. Blount. 1623.

The verses are printed above as they appear in the first edition. They are certainly not of a high order of merit, but quite in accordance with the spirit of the time when they were written.

Droeshout engraved a number of plates, among which may be mentioned portraits of John Fox; John Howson, Bishop of Durham; William Fairfax, and Lord Mountjoy Blount. His portrait of Shakespeare, however, while exhibiting the same hard, stiff style, is the worst of them all.

As the same plate was used in the four folio editions, it became more worn with each successive edition, until, in the fourth, it was very much poorer than in the first. Bohn says that the print, as it appeared in the first edition "is distinguishable from subsequent impressions by the shading on the left of the forehead (as it stands before you), which is expressed by single lines curving inwards from left to right without any crossing whatever, while in the repaired state, as it occurs in the fourth edition, the lines are strongly crossed, and bend outwards. Besides this, the hair is crossed in the repaired state, while in the original it is in single lines."*

The opinions of critics as to the merits of Droeshout's engraving have been various, but it has failed to receive a hearty commendation from any of them.

---

* *Lowndes' Bibliographer's Manual*, etc. Edited by Bohn. London: 1863, 8vo., p. 2255.

George Steevens says: "The verses in praise of Droeshout's performance were probably written as soon as they were bespoke, and before their author had an opportunity or inclination to compare the plate with its original. * * * * It is lucky indeed for those to whom metrical recommendations are necessary, that custom does not require they should be delivered upon oath. It is likewise probable that Ben Jonson had no acquaintance with the graphick art, and might not have been oversolicitous about the style in which Shakespeare's lineaments were transmitted to posterity."

John Britton, the antiquary, endorses what Steevens says, and adds that he cannot express his opinions better than by quoting Steevens' language, which he accordingly does.*

Boaden, on the other hand, thinks that "this portrait exhibits an aspect of calm benevolence and tender thought; great comprehension, and a kind of mixt feeling, as when melancholy yields to the suggestions of fancy." He further relates that Mr. Kemble, the celebrated actor, was much pleased with it.†

Wivell's opinion is also favorable, and he thinks that this engraving has the "most indubitable right to origi-

---

* *Appendix to Britton's Auto-Biography*, etc. London: 1850, 8vo., p. 18.
† *An Inquiry*, etc. London: 1824, 8vo., p. 17.

nality. It is, as I may say, the key to unlock and detect almost all the impositions that have, at various times, arrested so much of public attention. It is a witness that can refute all false evidence, and will satisfy every discerner how to appreciate and how to convict."*

Friswell says that the engraving is "not a skilful one, nor does it leave a very pleasing image on the beholder. * * * * * The eyes are peculiar; they are hardly fellows, but are not altogether ill drawn, and have about them a worn and hard-worked look. The cheeks are full and round; the hair straight, and turned under at the ears, which are without rings; the lip is long, and the moustache grows under each nostril, leaving a complete division as in the bust. * * * We may therefore, after weighing the evidence carefully, and taking into consideration the probabilities of the case, assume that the most authentic representation of the poet is that of the head attached to the First Folio of 1623, and that we may take it, together with the bust at Stratford-upon-Avon, as a test of the genuineness of the many other assumed portraits of the poet."†

Dr. Ingleby is of opinion that "next in authenticity to the bust is Droeshout's engraving, prefixed to the First

---

* *An Inquiry*, etc. London: 1827, 8vo., p. 56.
† *Life Portraits*, etc. London: 1864, 8vo., pp. 40, 42, and 45.

Folio edition of Shakespeare's Works. It must have been executed after Shakespeare's death; and therefore we may be sure it was taken from some sketch or painting, probably in the possession of Mrs. Shakespeare or Dr. John Hall. * * * * * Even in its best state it is such a monstrosity, that I, for one, do not believe that it had any trustworthy exemplar."*

J. O. Halliwell-Phillipps thinks that "although the defects in the drawing are painfully apparent, yet as being in all probability a copy from a genuine original picture, it is entitled to respectful consideration. Making allowances for inaccurate proportions, there appears to me to be a sufficient similarity between the bust and the print to lead to the conclusion that both are authentic and confirmatory of each other."†

It will be seen that while some critics find nothing to admire, others think quite favorably of this portrait. It certainly has no claim to rank very high as a work of art, and it strikes many people at first sight as unlike any human being; but long familiarity with it makes one first tolerate, and then grow to like it. It is as well authenticated as the Stratford bust, for Ben Jonson's testimony is of the highest value. He knew Shakespeare

---

* *Shakespeare: the Man, and the Book.* London: 1877, 4to., pp. 81, 83.
† *The Works of William Shakespeare,* etc. London: 1853, folio, Vol. I, p. 237.

well, and loved him too, in spite of what his detractors have tried to show. It is not probable, therefore, that Jonson would have given such a high testimonial to its merit as a likeness if it had not been so. Probably its faults are all to be laid at the door of Martin Droeshout. It is deeply to be regretted that the publishers of the First Folio did not select a better engraver.

It is, of course, impossible to say from what Droeshout engraved his plate, but it is more than probable that it was from some painting. Steevens believed at one time that he had found the original of this engraving in the Felton portrait (and it certainly bears a great resemblance to the latter), but the pedigree of that picture is so defective that it is more than probable that the Felton portrait was copied from the Droeshout engraving many years after the publication of the latter.

Droeshout's engraving is supposed by many to represent Shakespeare in a theatrical costume, with a stage wig. Indeed, critics have even gone so far as to suggest that it represented him in the character of Old Knowell in Ben Jonson's play of *Every Man in his Humour*, in which Shakespeare is known to have acted. It has also been further suggested that if this were so it would help to explain Ben Jonson's warm commendation of the engraving. While very ingenious, of course these are only conjectures.

Mr. J. O. Halliwell-Phillipps possesses an impression of the Droeshout engraving in a different state from any in which it appeared in the four folio editions. He thus describes it, in a privately printed catalogue of his engravings, etc.:

"The engraved head of Shakespeare on the title-page of the first collective edition of his Plays, 1623, Martin Droeshout sculpsit, London. *The original engraving by Droeshout before it was altered by an inferior hand, of extreme rarity, and the earliest engraved portrait of Shakespeare in existence.*

"No writers on the subject have suspected that the engraved portrait of Shakespeare, by Droeshout, 1623, has hitherto been accessible to them and to the public only in a vitiated form.

"A very superficial comparison of this original impression, with the print in its ordinary state, will suffice to establish the wide difference of appearance between the two impressions, a difference so great as to present an absolute variation of expression. But a long and attentive examination will be required before all the minute points of difference will be observed. Amongst these may be specially mentioned one in the left eyebrow of the portrait, which, in the original, is shaded from left to right, whereas, in the other, it is shaded from right to left. In the latter, under the shading can be traced, with the aid of the magnifying glass, portions of the earlier work, a fact decisively proving that the engraving was altered, perhaps by some inferior hand, into the form hitherto generally seen.

"The following observations upon the present copy of the engraving were kindly communicated by my late friend, F. W. Fairholt, F.S.A. 'The portrait, in this state of the engraving, is remarkable for clearness of tone; the shadows being very delicately rendered, so that the light falls upon the muscles of the face with a softness not to be found in the ordinary impressions. This is particularly visible in the arch under the eye, and in the muscles of the mouth; the expression of the latter is much altered in the later states of the plate by the enlargement of the upturned moustache, which hides and destroys the true character of this part of the face. The whole of the shadows have been darkened by cross-hatching and coarse dotting, particularly on the chin; this gives a coarse and undue prominence to some parts of the portrait, the forehead particularly. In this early state of the plate the hair is darker than any of the shadows on the head, and flows softly and naturally; in the retouched plate the shadow is much darker than the roots of the hair, imparting a swelled look to the head, and giving the hair the appearance of a raised wig. It is remarkable that no shadow falls across the collar; this omission, and the general low tone of color in the engraving, may have induced the retouching and strengthening which has injured the true character of the likeness, which, in its original state, is far more worthy of Ben Jonson's commendatory lines.'

"Mr. William Smith, whose knowledge of early engravings is unrivalled, thus writes, in reference to a suggestion that the variations were caused by an accident to the plate,—'I was unwilling to answer your note until I had made another careful examination of your engraving, as well as of the very fine impression in the usual state which we have recently purchased for the National Portrait Gallery. This I have now done, and I can find no traces of any damage whatever. I fully believe that, on what is technically termed *proving* the plate, it was thought that much of the work was so delicate as not to allow of a sufficient number of impressions being printed. Droeshout might probably have refused to spoil his work, and it was retouched by an inferior and coarser engraver.'"*

---

* *A Catalogue of a small portion of the Engravings and Drawings Illustrative of the Life of Shakespeare, preserved in the collection formed by J. O. Halliwell, Esq., F.R.S.* London: 1868, 8vo., p. 35.

When Mr. William Page, of New York, was studying the subject of Shakespeare's portraits, with a view to preparing his portrait and bust of Shakespeare, he was very anxious to see a photograph of Mr. Halliwell-Phillipps' unique impression of the Droeshout engraving, and the present writer was glad to be able to be the means of procuring him one from that gentleman.

Of this Mr. Page writes as follows: "I must record in this connection how the Halliwell Droeshout differs from the usually known print in the First Folio of 1623. I cannot do better than refer to Mr. Halliwell's views, as expressed in his 'Catalogue of a Small Portion of the Engravings and Drawings Illustrative of the Life of Shakespeare, preserved in the Collection formed by J. O. Halliwell-Phillipps, Esq., F.R.S., etc. Printed for Private Reference.' My attention was called to this unique Droeshout by an extract from this 'Catalogue' in an article on the portraits of Shakespeare, by J. Parker Norris, Esq., of Philadelphia, who also finally procured me a full-sized photograph of the same from Mr. Halliwell.

"I have carefully compared the photographs of this Halliwell Droeshout with the two prints from the same plate in the Astor Library, the darker one from the collection of the Duke of Buckingham. Mr. Halliwell's is evidently an earlier impression from the same plate before it was retouched and used for the other known impressions in the First Folio of 1623. The differences which Mr. Halliwell points out are very obvious. In the impressions from the retouched plate in the Astor Library, the lights and darks are generally emphasized at the expense of characterization. Whoever retouched the plate, in his mistaken efforts to improve the general effect, lost markings, modellings, accents all over the face. Yet this darker impression in the Astor Library must have been an uncommonly good one after the retouchings mentioned. But character is lost in the left temple, lost utterly in the differences in the eyebrows, so evident in the Halliwell Droeshout, and identified in the Stratford bust and the Death Mask. In the retouched plate the eyebrows are evened over and brought to the prim precision which the latter workman aimed at. Quite a thorough-going line is carried over both eyebrows, which, in the earlier impression, was much more delicate and individual. The new workman had a praiseworthy intention also in adding the shadow upon the collar, which did not exist at all in the earlier state of the plate. That it was the same plate may be known from the accidents in it, repeated in all the impressions by a little black spot under the nose and at the corner of the mouth. I say *accidents*, because there is no evidence of lines being laid by the graving tool to represent such markings in the original from which the portrait was taken. They are caused by bad places in the metal of the plate. The peculiar marking or corrugation of the left eyebrow, as indication of a certain peculiar marking between the nose and the hairs of the brow of the actual person, is all lost in the retouched plate. * * * * * The meaning of the Halliwell Droeshout is more evident, and the original lines laid with more truth to nature in the original intention. I have submitted my photograph of it to experts in engraving and corrected my impressions, when necessary, in regard to what was intentional by the artist and rendered by the graving tool, and what was accidental to the plate or to the impression from it."*

The present writer also sent, by request, a photograph of the Halliwell-Phillipps' unique impression of the Droeshout engraving to Mr. Lenox, of New York, the founder of the Lenox Library, to whom the public owes so much for his noble gift, which will carry his name down to all time. In acknowledging its receipt, he wrote as follows, under date of August 24, 1874:

"I have just received, and hasten to offer my acknowledgments for, the photographic likeness of Shakespeare. It enables me to understand, better than I did,

---

* *A Study of Shakespeare's Portraits.* London: 1876, 48mo., p. 33.

Mr. Halliwell's remarks in his 'Catalogue of Engravings Illustrative of Shakespeare,' though I cannot yet comprehend the whole of them. Compared with the portrait in my copies of the Folio, 1623, I can see no difference in the *shading of the left eyebrow, etc.*, but the *upturned moustache* is enlarged, and there are more lines in my copies for the shading of the forehead. Indeed, these seem to be intermediate between Mr. H.'s and those subsequently struck off. Yet as a whole, mine, and especially Harris's fac-simile, are softer and clearer than your photograph—a difference owing probably to the photograph and not perhaps in the original.

"On examining my volume I unexpectedly found a cutting from one of Lilly's catalogues, which I had probably put into the volume for the purpose of examination and forgotten. I copy it:

"Lilly's catalogue of rare, curious, useful books, page 112 (date not known.) * * *

"'A perfect copy of this precious volume. The portrait is in a unique state, before the shading on the left side of the laced collar, but imprint below is in fac-simile.'

"In my copies the 'laced collar' on Shakespeare's left side is different from your photograph. There *is* a shading from the chin up to the hair."

In 1640 there was published a work entitled: "Poems.

MARSHALL'S COPY OF

The Droeshout Engraving.

FROM AN OLD ENGRAVING.

This Shadowe is renowned Shakespear's Soule of th' age
The applause? delight! the wonder of the Stage.
Nature her selfe, was proud of his designes
And joy'd to weare the dressing of his lines,
The learned will Confess, his works are such,
As neither man, nor Muse, can prayse to much.
For ever live thy fame, the world to tell,
Thy like, no age, shall ever paralell.

W. M. sculpsit.

Written by Wil. Shake-speare, Gent. Printed at London by Tho. Cotes, and are to be sold by Iohn Benson, dwelling in St. Dunstan's Church-yard. 1640." In this book appeared a plate, consisting of a portrait of Shakespeare, copied from the Droeshout picture, but changed in many details. It was engraved by W. Marshall.

In copying the Droeshout plate Marshall has turned the head in the opposite direction, and added to the length of the figure so as to show the left arm, with the hand covered with a gauntlet, and holding a branch of laurel. Over the right shoulder is a cloak. The whole is enclosed in an oval frame. Marshall's engraving presents a worse appearance than Droeshout's.

Droeshout's engraving has been reproduced by many subsequent engravers, generally with indifferent results. They all seem to have tried to improve the original engraving, and having nothing but their fancy to guide them in their efforts to do so, the results have not been satisfactory.

The first copy from Droeshout's plate is supposed to have been engraved by W. Fairthorne, and was published in 1655. It is in an oval about an inch and a half long, which is at the top of a picture representing a woman stabbing herself, while a man looks on too astonished to stop her. Underneath the plate are the following lines:

> *"The Fates decree, that tis a mighty wrong*
> *To Woemen Kinde, to have more Greife, then Tongue*
>
> Will: Gilbirson: John Stafford excud."

The head of Shakespeare is reversed, but is a fair copy of the original.

The early editions of Shakespeare (apart from the four folios, which, as has before been stated, contained the original Droeshout engraving), did not reproduce this picture of the poet, but quite a good copy appeared in Johnson and Steevens' edition of Shakespeare, published in 1778. No engraver's name is given.

An engraving published by J. Bell, September 5, 1786, (no engraver's name,) in Bell's edition of Shakespeare is next in order. It is a poor performance, and gives but a faint idea of the original.

W. Sherwin engraved a plate for John Stockdale, which was published September 1, 1790. The entire expression is changed, and it is about as poor a copy as can well be imagined.

The above print must not be confounded with one engraved by H. Brocas, and published by William Jones, in 1791. Brocas states that it is "from the original Folio Edition," but he evidently copied Sherwin's print of the year before instead. It closely resembles the latter in appearance and in the manner of its engraving, and has all of the faults of Sherwin's plate.

When Ireland gave to the world his wretched forgeries, which he succeeded in palming off on many men (who should have known better) as original MS. by Shakespeare, Samuel Ireland engraved, Dec. 1, 1795, the miserable drawing which bears some slight resemblance to the Droeshout; but it is so badly executed that it looks like the work of a child. It was published in the *Miscellaneous Papers*, etc., London: 1796.

In 1807 a reprint of the First Folio was issued. It contained a good copy of Droeshout's print, but it is better engraved than his plate, and the expression softened. No engraver's name is given.

In 1819 R. Sawyer copied the plate supposed to have been engraved by W. Fairthorne, and which is referred to above. This copy was subsequently given among the illustrations in Wivell's *Inquiry*, in 1827.

Thurston drew a very poor copy of Droeshout's picture, which was engraved by Rivers, and published by Sherwin & Co., in 1821. In this print the expression of the face is much altered, and it is entirely unlike the original.

J. Swaine was much more successful in his copy, published in Boaden's *Inquiry*, London: 1824, 8vo., but he has softened the expression very materially, and the lower part of the face is too dark. This plate was also used in Harness' Shakespeare, Vol. I, London: 1830, 8vo.

A small engraving by Augustus Fox was published in Pickering's miniature edition of Shakespeare, London: 1825, 48mo. It is fair.

The same year (1825,) Pickering also published a larger plate, engraved by W. H. Worthington. The workmanship on the plate is very good, but the resemblance to Droeshout's engraving is slight.

In 1827 Wivell gave the best copy of the original engraving that had then been published. It is engraved by C. Picart, and accompanied Wivell's *Inquiry*, London: 1827, 8vo. The background, however, and also the face, is not engraved in the same manner as Droeshout's picture.

About this time W. Smith, of London, published quite a good copy of Droeshout's engraving. There is no date, or engraver's name, on the plate, and Ben Jonson's lines "To the Reader," are underneath. It is engraved in imitation of Droeshout's rough manner, and is very meritorious.

Collier's first edition of Shakespeare, Vol. I, London: 1844, 8vo., contains a plate engraved by H. Cook, which is a fair copy of the original. This same plate is used in Collier's edition of Shakespeare, published in one volume, 4to, London: 1853, and also in his edition in six volumes, 8vo, London: 1858.

Henry Rumsey Forster's *Few Remarks*, etc., London: 1849, 8vo., has a small engraving of the head of the Droeshout, which is very well done, but the beard is too dark.

T. H. Lacy published, in 1857, a volume entitled *The Legend of Shakespeare's Crab Tree*, by Green, which contained quite a fair copy of the Droeshout. The engraver's name is not given, and this is to be regretted, as the print is a very striking one.

To engrave a copy of the Droeshout on wood is a very difficult feat, and it has never been successfully accomplished. It was tried by G. Dalziel, for Knight's Cabinet edition of Shakespeare, and the result was an utter failure. A wood-cut published in Grant White's Shakespeare, Vol. II, Boston: 1858, 8vo., was better; but when Lionel Booth issued his prospectus for his admirable reprint of the First Folio, it contained a very poor engraving on wood from the Droeshout. Lastly, W. J. Linton engraved quite a large copy on wood, which was presented to the subscribers to Cassell's Illustrated Shakespeare. It is well engraved, but entirely different from the original.

An engraving by H. Robinson, with Shakespeare's autograph under it, published about 1860, possesses some merit, and is well engraved, but the expression is changed. It appeared in the Lansdowne edition of Shakespeare.

The first accurate reproduction of Droeshout's picture was one made by the photo-zincographic process—at the Ordnance Survey Office, Southampton, under the direction of Sir Henry James, in 1862. The cross hatching on the face and in the background has come out rather too dark, but on the whole it is very satisfactory. A complete fac-simile of the title-page of the First Folio is given.

A small, though very good photo-lithograph of the print appeared in Lionel Booth's reprint of the First Folio, London: 1864, in the quarto and small quarto editions of that book, but in the folio one a photograph is given.

Dr. Leo's edition of *Coriolanus*, London: 1864, 4to., p. 128, contains a good photo-lithograph of the Droeshout. An excellent photograph of it appeared in Friswell's *Life Portraits*, etc., London: 1864, 8vo. Kenny's *Life and Genius of Shakespeare*, London: 1864, 8vo., has a fair copy, but no engraver's name is given.

Photographs of Droeshout's engraving are not generally successful, as the cross hatching so extensively used by Droeshout does not come out clear in the negative, and the yellowish tint of the paper of the original folio causes a general darkness of tone in the print, which is not satisfactory; but an admirable one, by Preston, was published by Day & Son, in Staunton's *Memorials of Shakespeare*, London: 1864, folio; and a splendid photo-lithograph was published by the same firm April 9, 1864. This is from the print in the First Folio belonging to the Earl of Ellesmere, and is a superb copy of a brilliant impression of the engraving. This photo-lithograph was also used in Staunton's photo-lithographic reproduction of the First Folio, London: 1866.

A series of four photographs, made from copies of the First, Second, Third, and Fourth Folios, belonging to the Barton collection, in the Boston Public Library, are in the possession of the present writer. They prove what has been before said about photographs of this engraving from the originals being seldom satisfactory.

Mary Cowden Clarke's Edition of Shakespeare, Vol. I, New York: 1866, royal 8vo., contained a poor copy by J. C. Armytage.

A plate by R. C. Bell in Clarke's Shakespeare, London: 1869, 4to., is much better.

The heliotype reproductions in Justin Winsor's *Bibliography of the Quartos and Folios*, etc., Boston: 1876, folio, are very unsatisfactory. They are from the copies in the Barton collection.

A fairly good photo-lithograph appeared in Halliwell-

Phillipps' fac-simile of the First Folio, published by Chatto & Windus, London: 1876, 8vo.

A wood-cut of this print in the Leopold Shakespeare, London: 1877, 4to., and another in the Avon edition of the poet's works, Philadelphia: 1879, royal 8vo., fall under the objection to wood-cut copies of this engraving above referred to.

In 1882 the New Shakespeare Society published a photograving by the Typographic Etching Company of London. The lines in this copy are too heavy, and there is a general effect of blackness which is very unsatisfactory.

Marshall's plate has been frequently copied. A good copy was published in Johnson & Steevens' edition of Shakespeare, Vol. I, London: 1778, 8vo., and the same plate was used in the edition of 1785.

A poor plate, by Delattre, was published in Bell's Shakespeare, London: 1786, 16mo.

A copy utterly unlike Marshall's was engraved by H. Adlard, and published by Wetton & Jarvis, Dec. 1, 1821.

An excellent engraving was published in Boaden's *Inquiry*, London: 1824, 8vo., and the same plate was used in Wivell's *Inquiry*, London: 1827, 8vo.

A well engraved copy by H. Robinson was published in Pickering's edition of Shakespeare, London: 1832, 16mo.

The Chandos Portrait.

FROM MEZZOTINT BY COUSINS.

THE CHANDOS PORTRAIT.

PERHAPS the best known of all the portraits professing to represent Shakespeare is the Chandos. Certainly it is the most familiar to the large mass of people. The cheap plaster cast, hawked about the streets by the Italian image vender, is modelled after this portrait, while the handsome bronze that one puts over his clock has the same features. In a word, the Chandos is the popularly accepted representation of Shakespeare. How this has come about it would be difficult to say, unless it be that the public would not have the Stratford bust or the Droeshout engraving. They are the only ones well authenticated, but they have not met with popular favor like the Chandos, whose pedigree is very unsatisfactory.

This picture was first heard of towards the end of the seventeenth century, after the year 1683, when Sir Godfrey Kneller made a copy of it for Dryden. This is the first fact that we know concerning it. It has an elaborate pedigree, however, which must now be discussed.

It is not known by whom it was painted. Some critics have believed that it was the work of Richard Burbage, the actor. He possessed considerable skill as an artist, and in Dulwich College there is still preserved a portrait of himself which he painted. The style and manner of the work in this portrait of Burbage, are said to be similar to the Chandos picture.

Joseph Taylor, an actor, is reputed to have been its first owner, but whether he purchased it from Burbage, or it was given to him by the latter, tradition is silent. He is supposed to have left it by will to Sir William D'Avenant, but no will of Taylor's has been found, and as the latter was extremely poor, this is not a happy conjecture.

There is a tradition that Sir William D'Avenant owned this picture, but here again there is not a particle of proof. If it could be established as a fact that D'Avenant really did own this portrait, it would be much in favor of its authenticity. Sir William was reputed to have been Shakespeare's natural son, and the possession of his father's portrait would have been probable in the case of one who was proud of being thought to have had Shakespeare's blood in his veins.

D'Avenant died in 1668, and appears to have owed a considerable amount of money. Administration of his effects was granted to John Otway, in that year, who was his principal creditor. It was possibly at the sale of D'Avenant's effects that Betterton purchased the Chandos portrait; and while it was in the latter's possession it was engraved by Vander Gucht, for Rowe's edition of Shakespeare, published in 1709.

When Betterton died he was a poor man, and his collection of portraits of actors and others were sold. Mrs. Barry, the actress, purchased the Chandos portrait at that sale, and she afterwards sold it to Robert Keck, of the Temple, London, for forty guineas.

A Mr. Nicoll, Nicholl, or Nicholls was the next owner (his name is spelled in a variety of ways by different writers). He married into the Keck family, and the portrait thus came into his possession; and when his daughter married James, Marquis of Caernarvon, who was afterwards Duke of Chandos, it became the latter's property. From the latter nobleman it takes its name. The Duke of Chandos' daughter was Anna Eliza, Duchess of Buckingham, and she inherited the picture from her father.

At the sale of the Duke of Buckingham's pictures at Stowe, in September, 1848, this portrait was sold for three hundred and fifty-five guineas, to the Earl of Ellesmere. The latter nobleman presented it in March, 1856, to the National Portrait Gallery, where it now remains.

In the catalogue of that collection the history of the Chandos portrait is thus given:

"The Chandos Shakespeare was the property of John Taylor, the player,* by whom, or by Richard Burbage, it was painted. The picture was left by the former, in his will, to Sir William D'Avenant.† After his death it was bought by Betterton, the actor, upon whose decease Mr. Keck, of the Temple, purchased it for forty guineas, from whom it was inherited by Mr. Nicholls, of Michendon House, Southgate, Middlesex, whose only daughter married James, Marquis of Caernarvon, afterwards Duke of Chandos, father to Anna Eliza, Duchess of Buckingham."

It will be noticed that the above history omits the ownership of the picture by Mrs. Barry; and while it gives the picture's pedigree as if there was very little doubt about it, there is no authority brought forward to substantiate the statements therein contained.

---

* The John Taylor referred to here is probably a mistake for Joseph Taylor, as there was no John Taylor who was an actor. Perhaps, however, John Taylor, the painter, is intended. He painted two portraits of Taylor, the Water poet, which are in the Picture Gallery at Oxford. They bear the inscription "*John Taylor pinx. 1655*," and are said to be painted in the same style as the Chandos portrait.

† There is no authority whatever for this statement.

Such is the pedigree of this famous portrait. It will be seen that very little is positively known regarding it, but that much that has been given above is founded on mere statements and conjectures. In length and in containing celebrated names its pedigree is far ahead of either the Stratford bust or the Droeshout engraving, but while they are perfectly well authenticated, this portrait's pedigree is largely made up of allegations not capable of proof.

Betterton's ownership, as before stated, is the first positive fact in its history, if we except the circumstance of its having been copied by Kneller a short time previous to this, and it is not even known who owned the picture when the latter copied it.

When Kneller presented his copy of the picture to Dryden, the latter sent the painter, in return, some verses commencing:

> "Shakespeare, thy gift, I place before my sight,
> With awe I ask his blessing as I write;
> With reverence look on his majestick face,
> Proud to be less, but of his godlike race.
> His soul inspires me, while thy praise I write,
> And I like Teucer under Ajax fight:
> Bids thee, through me, be bold; with dauntless breast
> Contemn the bad, and emulate the best:
> Like his, thy criticks in the attempt are lost,
> When most they rail, know then, they envy most."

Dryden's copy of the portrait afterwards came into the possession of Earl Fitzwilliam, of Wentworth House, and Dr. Waagen, in the *Art Treasures of Great Britain*, thus speaks of it:

"A portrait of Shakespeare, a copy made by Sir Godfrey Kneller, and by him presented to Dryden, is only so far interesting as showing the same features as those in the Chandos picture (now, 1855) in the Bridgewater Gallery, thus corroborating the truth of that portrait."

Sir Joshua Reynolds is stated to have made a copy of the Chandos portrait in 1760, for Bishop Newton; and an anonymous copy was presented by Edward Capell to Trinity College, Cambridge.

After the picture had been purchased by the Earl of Ellesmere, John Payne Collier read a paper concerning it, before the old Shakespeare Society, exhibiting the portrait to the members at the same time. Mr. Collier inclined to the belief that it was painted by Richard Burbage, the actor, who possessed some skill in painting. Burbage's portrait, painted by himself, which is at Dulwich College, Mr. Collier thought bore evidence of having been painted in a similar manner. This has been denied, however, by H. Rodd, who was a good judge of old pictures. He says that both pictures are of the one period, that they have both been carelessly cleaned, and that they have both been retouched; but the portrait of Burbage is not well drawn or colored, and as a work of art it does not compare well with the Chandos portrait. Rodd believed that the latter was painted by Cornelius Jansen. This is not probable, however, as he is supposed not to have come to England before 1618, when he took up his residence in Blackfriars. The truth is, the painter of the Chandos portrait is not known, and, it is only reasonable to presume, he never will be.

After Mr. Collier had read his paper before the old Shakespeare Society *The Athenæum* contained an anonymous article, in which Mr. Collier's statement that the portrait was painted by Burbage is doubted, and the copy of Oldy's notes to Langbaine, (on which authority Mr. Collier founded his belief,) is thus given entire:

"Mr. Nicholas [Nicholl] of Southgate has a picture of Shakespeare which they say was painted by old Cornelius Jansen, others by Rich. Burbage the player.

"Mr. Keck of the Temple gave Mrs. Barry 40 guineas for her Shakespeare—the same."

Little or no weight must be attached to Oldy's statements, for it will be noticed that he gives the names of two persons who are said to have painted the picture—Cornelius Jansen and Richard Burbage—and allows the reader to take his choice.

The writer of the *Athenæum* article states that he believes the present Chandos portrait to be a copy of the picture painted by Burbage, but fails to give any reason for thinking so. He also believes that this picture was copied for D'Avenant, and that it belonged to him "beyond the possibility of doubt," but, as before stated, there is no authority whatever for this allegation.

The portrait is twenty-two inches high and eighteen inches wide. It is on canvas, and is painted in an oval, representing stone, and the background is of a reddish brown. The inner edge of this oval has a reflected light in one part of it, to represent the thickness of the stone. This gives somewhat of a yellowish tinge surrounding the head, and has been referred to by some writers to show that this portrait is a copy of the date of Kneller's pictures, that being a characteristic of the latter. In reality, however, there is no such yellowness around the head as these writers have claimed; indeed, the whole background is so dark that it is necessary to have a good light to see what its color is.

George Scharf, F.S.A., and an artist of some repute, contributed a valuable and interesting paper on *The Principal Portraits of Shakespeare* to *Notes and Queries* for April 23, 1864. This admirable, though brief, essay was subsequently reprinted in book form, in 16mo., in the same year. On page 8 Mr. Scharf thus gives his opinion of this portrait: "It is painted on coarse English canvas, covered with a groundwork of greenish gray, which has been rubbed bare in several parts, where the coarse threads of the canvas happen most to project. Only a few parts of the face have been retouched with a reddish paint. Some portions of the hair seem to have been darkened, and a few touches of deep madder red may have been added to give point to the nostrils and eyelids. The background is a rich dark red; but the whole tone of the picture has become blackened, partly in consequence of the gray ground protruding, and partly from the red colors of the flesh tints having deepened to a brownish tone. This at first sight gives the complexion a dull swarthy hue. The features are well modelled, and the shadows skilfully massed, so as to produce a portrait in no way unworthy of the time of Van Somer and Cornelius Jansen. It would be folly to speculate upon the name of the artist, but any one conversant with pictures of this period would, upon careful examination, pronounce it remarkably good if only the production of an amateur."

Sir Joshua Reynolds is said to have been of the opinion that the Chandos portrait was left in an unfinished state by the artist, but Mr. Rodd, in a letter to

Mr. Forster, says that Sir Joshua could never have held this opinion, and attributes this peculiar appearance to too frequent and injudicious cleaning. He continues: "Sir Joshua must have known that neither the ancient nor the modern masters finished the borders, and the more minute details and subordinate parts of their pictures, before they had completed the face. The oval border and the dark red colored background of the picture in question have not only been highly finished, but are now very pure, and, with the exception of a slight damage over the head, it is not retouched or 'painted over.' The face, hair, and dress have suffered more or less by an unskilful cleaner. Whoever was the person intrusted to clean it, he must have used a strong alkali, as the finish and glazing of the face are much damaged, and even the collar, which, being nearly all composed of white lead, is more durable, has materially suffered; the most remarkable thing is, that the mouth still remains perfect, and sweetly beautiful it is! The dress has suffered; but there is sufficient of the picture left—the outline being perfect—for a skilful repairer to connect the whole, not by 'painting over,' but by stippling in the small particles with paint or water-color, where rubbed off, to match the parts left. The head is finely drawn and well colored, the face has an expression of intelligence and vivacity, and there is not one point in it leading us to doubt its originality."*

In 1783 Malone had a careful drawing made from the original picture by Ozias Humphry, whom he styles an "excellent artist." Speaking of this copy Malone (in 1784) said: "The original having been painted by a very ordinary hand, having been at some subsequent period painted over, and being now in a state of decay, this copy, which is a very faithful one, is in my opinion invaluable."

Steevens (who termed this portrait the D'Avenantico-Bettertono-Barryan-Keckian-Nicholsian-Chandosan canvas,) says, in his preface to the 1793 edition of the poet's works, that the reason that that edition contains no portrait of Shakespeare is because "the only portrait of him that even pretends to authenticity, by means of injudicious cleaning, or some other accident, has become little better than the 'shadow of a shade.' * * * * * Of the drapery and curling hair exhibited in the excellent engravings of Mr. Vertue, Mr. Hall, and Mr. Knight, the painting does not afford a vestige; nor is there a feature or circumstance on the whole canvas, that can with minute precision be delineated."

---

* *A Few Remarks*, etc. London: 1849, 8vo., p. 18.

William Page says: "Let us look next to the Chandos portrait, painted probably twelve or fourteen years after the Droeshout. Whatever shortcomings the picture contains, I think it was painted by a man of the craft, and one who had committed like artistic sins so many times as to fix a habit or *manner* of not doing it. * * * * I repeat, we are indebted to the Arundel Society's photographs for all we can know of any of its claims to any characteristic likeness to nature or to Shakespeare. In the National Portrait Gallery it is almost a complete negation, its cleanings and mendings leaving the expert scarcely a foothold in his search for the original picture."*

The Arundel Society photograph from the original picture, referred to above, by Mr. Page, represents the portrait in a very dilapidated condition. The stone arch surrounding the portrait has almost entirely disappeared, the head has nearly faded out of sight, and the white collar is the one distinct thing to be seen in the whole picture. Desiring to know whether this photograph represented the picture as it now is, the present writer requested Dr. C. M. Ingleby, (who has given much time and attention to the subject of Shakespeare's portraits) to state his views on this point. Under date of November 13, 1883, he very kindly wrote as follows:

---

* *A Study of Shakespeare's Portraits.* London: 1876, 24mo., p. 40.

"Conformably to your request, I went, yesterday, to the National Portrait Gallery, taking with me the Arundel Society's photograph of the Chandos portrait of Shakespeare, and I beg to report to you as follows:

"The photograph does not give the least notion of the original, which is a carefully finished picture, exhibiting none of the dilapidation shown in the photograph.

"If I may trust my recollection of the portrait when it first left the collection of Lord Francis Egerton,* I should say that the picture has been restored since it became national property. When I first saw it, it was in very bad condition, the cracks in the varnish marring the painting. The cracks are still visible on close inspection, but they have been varnished over. I believe the photograph to have been made before the restoration of the picture, but of this I cannot be sure, as the reds come up so badly in a photograph, and not improbably, the picture was not removed from the glass which protects it. I could discover nothing in it to account for the dreadful mess in the nose and mouth in the photograph.

"The portrait in its present condition is represented, with the utmost accuracy, in Samuel Cousins' mezzotint."

Dr. Ingleby wrote to Mr. George Scharf, the Curator

---

* The Earl of Ellesmere.

of the National Portrait Gallery, asking whether the portrait had been cleaned or restored. Mr. Scharf replied that it had not been cleaned or even varnished, so far as he could remember, and that the portrait was in a good state of preservation, and did not need anything done to it.

How then can the Arundel Society's photograph be explained? The portrait could not have been in the condition it is now when that photograph was taken, or it would have made a much better copy than that shows. Compare, too, what Malone, Steevens, Rodd, Friswell, Scharf, and Page say about the state of the portrait.

It is to be feared that the picture has been "restored," as it is called, that is, painted over so as to cover over much of the original work.

The Chandos portrait is more like the Stratford bust than the Droeshout engraving, but many persons fail to find any resemblance between either of these authentic portraits and the subject of the present essay. It has a very Jewish face, and the ear-rings give it a foreign look, although it was not uncommon for Englishmen of Shakespeare's day to wear them. It is a most disappointing picture, and those bronzes and engravings which have been copied from it, and received by the public as ideal likenesses of the poet, owe their popularity to the skill of the artists who made them, and not to a literal rendering of the original picture, which is most unsatisfactory.

Boaden thought very favorably of this picture, and seems to have believed in its authenticity. He was much impressed with Malone's acceptance of it as a genuine portrait of the poet.

Friswell says: "The picture, which is in oil, and on canvas, is at first glance disappointing. One cannot readily imagine our essentially English Shakespeare to have been a dark, heavy man, with a foreign expression, of a decidedly Jewish physiognomy, thin curly hair, a somewhat lubricious mouth, red-edged eyes, wanton lips, with a coarse expression, and his ears tricked out with ear-rings. The forehead has a somewhat noble aspect, but has been retouched by a clumsy restorer. The eyes are hardly well rendered in any print but that after Ozias Humphry, and those have a little exaggeration. They are of dark brown, and fixed in a thoughtful gaze. The eyes are full, and somewhat heavy, the supra-orbital ridge well developed and round, as it is in the bust—in the Houbraken portrait* it is flat. The hair, which is auburn inclining to dark brown, is in great profusion, the chin and upper lip fully covered with hair, the upper

---

* Friswell means Houbraken's engraving of the Chandos portrait, published in 1747.

lip very short, and totally different from that of the Stratford bust or the Droeshout portrait.

"The dress of the figure, so far as we are now able to distinguish, is of black satin, the collar of lawn, plain and simple, with white strings, which show through the beard, and are sewn over the collar. The painting has been very much scrubbed, and has been injured by injudicious cleaners and restorers."*

It has been conjectured that the Chandos portrait represents Shakespeare in the character of Shylock, and its Jewish appearance lends some weight to this supposition.

No portrait of Shakespeare has been so frequently engraved as the Chandos, and it will be impossible to do more than notice some of the most striking prints. The earliest plate is by M. Vander Gucht, and was published in the first edition of Rowe's Shakespeare, London: 1709, 8vo. It is in all of the volumes, and is in an oval, supported on a square pedestal. On either side are allegorical representations of Tragedy and Comedy, each holding a laurel wreath over the poet's head, and above is an allegorical picture of Fame. All the work on the plate is better than the portrait of the poet, which is quite insignificent in size, and poorly engraved. The

---

* *Life Portraits*, etc. London: 1864, 8vo., p. 31.

hair is much more curly than in the original picture, and the costume is much more prominent than it should in a copy of the Chandos portrait.

When Pope's edition of Shakespeare appeared in 1725, 4to., it contained a beautifully executed plate by G. Vertue, dated 1721, which had above it, on a ribbon, "William Shakespeare," and underneath, the arms of the poet on a small shield. The portrait purports to be a copy of the Chandos, but it is entirely unlike it, and the resemblance to the pictures of James I. is striking.

Theobald's Shakespeare, first edition, London: 1733, 8vo., contained a plate engraved by G. Duchange and drawn by B. Arlaud. It is totally unlike the original painting. The face is turned the other way; only a slight drooping moustache and goatee are given instead of the full beard in the original; the whole expression of the face is changed, and the dress is utterly unlike also. The portrait is in an oval, and underneath is the inscription, "Mr. William Shakespeare" in neat writing.

A copy of Duchange's plate, so far as the portrait is concerned, was engraved by Lud. du Guernier about this date, but the head is turned the correct way. The allegorical figures of Tragedy, Comedy, and Fame are the same in this plate as in M. Vander Gucht's, 1709.

Hanmer's Shakespeare, first edition, London: 1744,

4to., contained an engraving by H. Gravelot, which, though well engraved, is entirely different from the original. The head is turned the wrong way. In Hanmer's second edition, London: 1771, 4to., the same plate was used.

Houbraken engraved a large plate in an artistic manner, with the portrait in an oval, the head looking the wrong way, and beneath a group of musical instruments, a mask, etc. This was for Birch's *Heads of Illustrious Persons of Great Britain*, London: 1743–52, folio. The plate is dated 1747, and has been frequently copied by later engravers. It is very interesting, because it states that the original painting was then "in the possession of John Nicoll of Southgate," and fixes the date of his ownership.

G. Vertue engraved a print which was published in Warburton's edition of Shakespeare, London: 1747, 8vo. It has the head reversed. The hair is very curly, and the expression entirely different from the original. This print was used in Johnson's Shakespeare, first edition (London: 1765, 8vo.), and in his second edition (London: 1768, 8vo.); also in Johnson and Steevens' Shakespeare, first edition (London: 1773, 8vo.).

G. Vander Gucht engraved a plate, with the head reversed, which was used in the later editions of Theobald's Shakespeare, in 16mo, *e. g.* 1757, etc.

T. Cook copied Houbraken's engraving, but placed the head and figure the right way. It is a poor print and was published by G. Kearsley, *circa* 1770.

John Hall engraved a small plate in 1772, which is better than the preceding ones, but the head and figure are reversed and the expression changed.

Many of Jacob Tonson's publications, about this date, had on their title-pages a small wood-cut, badly executed, but evidently copied from Duchange's plate of 1733.

Johnson and Steevens' Shakespeare (London: 1785, 8vo.,) contained an engraving, by John Hall, which has evidently been made from the drawing by Ozias Humphry, in 1783, for Malone; and in Malone's Shakespeare (London: 1790, 8vo.,) appeared a plate engraved by C. Knight, from the same drawing, and dated 1786. There is a softness of expression and an idealization about Humphry's copy which is entirely wanting in the original, and yet Malone said that it was "a very faithful one."

Cook engraved another plate in 1788, for Bell's edition of Shakespeare, totally different from his engraving in *circa* 1770, and not at all like the original.

About this date a good engraving, but too dark, was made by Goldar. "William Shakespear" is at the top of the plate instead of in the usual place underneath.

A curious engraving, in an oval, with "W. Shakespear"

on the oval, and a poor one with "Wm. Shakespeare, Esqr.," at the bottom, both about this date, serve to show the infinite variety of expression given by each different engraver of this portrait.

N. Parr engraved a small oval plate very much like Duchange's, 1733. It was published *circa* 1790.

Holl engraved an oval plate, in dots, from Humphry's drawing, *circa* 1790, and about the same time an engraving by G. Vander Gucht, a son of M. Vander Gucht, was published. The work on it is coarse, but the resemblance to Duchange's plate (1733) is unmistakeable. This plate must not be confounded with the one by the same engraver published in Theobald's later editions of Shakespeare, *e. g.* 1757, etc. It closely resembles that engraving but it is different.

The *Universal Magazine*, *circa* 1790, contained an engraving copied from Houbraken's plate, which is very unsatisfactory. The expression has been changed, and Shakespeare is represented with a villainous countenance.

In 1793 Harding's *Shakespeare Illustrated*, etc., appeared. Among the numerous engravings in that work was one of the Chandos portrait, drawn by S. Harding and engraved by Le Goux. It is very poor.

Audinet engraved a plate, with the head reversed, published by Harrison & Co., March 1, 1794. It is from

Houbraken's engraving and is small, but the workmanship is very good.

Ireland's *Picturesque Views on the Upper, or Warwickshire Avon*, etc., London: 1795, 8vo., contained a poor plate drawn by Burney and engraved by C. Apostool; and another plate, copied from Houbraken's print, and well engraved, has "William Shakespear" in a circle surrounding it, which is divided into four parts. (No engraver's name. *Circa* 1800.)

A very curious mezzotint engraving, "printed for Robt. Sayer, Print Seller, No. 53 Fleet Street," bears very little resemblance to the Chandos portrait, and has a most villainous expression. Fortunately it is very scarce. (*Circa* 1800.)

Sharpe's edition of Shakespeare, London: 1803, 24mo., contained a poor print drawn by R. Corbould, and engraved by P. W. Tomkins.

S. Bennett engraved a plate, after Vertue's first print, (1721,) which was published by I. Stockdale, January 1, 1807; which is wretched. Vertue's print of 1721, it will be remembered, represented James I., while purporting to copy the Chandos portrait, and Bennett has feebly imitated the print.

Malone's Shakespeare, edited by Boswell, London: 1821, 8vo., contained a fair print, engraved by Fry.

Heath engraved a very poor copy of the Chandos, which was published by Jones & Co., May 4, 1822. At the top of the picture is an allegorical figure representing Fame about to crown the poet, and at the bottom are Comedy and Tragedy.

An edition of Shakespeare, published in ten volumes, London: 1823, 16mo., has a plate engraved by Dean, which is quite fair.

The best engraving after Ozias Humphry's drawing is that by Scriven, and published in Boaden's *Inquiry*, London: 1824, 8vo. It is the handsomest picture made from the Chandos, and by far the most intellectual one. It has been often copied by later engravers, but it is not a true representation of the Chandos portrait. It will always be sought for as a beautiful print, and one of Scriven's most successful works. The same plate was used in Harness' edition of Shakespeare, London: 1830, 8vo.

Singer's first edition of Shakespeare, London: 1826, 16mo., contained an engraving on wood by John Thompson, from a drawing by W. Harvey, which is well done, but not a good copy of the Chandos. It is surrounded by an emblematical border.

Wivell drew the best copy of the Chandos for his *Inquiry*, London: 1827, 8vo., that had then been published.

It was engraved by John Cochran, mainly in dots, and is an excellent specimen of his work.

Edward Smith engraved a well-executed plate for the Union Shakespeare, published by Robert Jennings, 1829. It is intended to be a copy of the Chandos, but the artist, whose name is not given, has utterly failed to give the slightest idea of the original.

A poor copy, engraved by Freeman, appeared in Valpy's Shakespeare, London: 1832, 16mo.

Wivell drew another copy of this portrait, which was engraved by W. Holl, and published by Thomas Kelly, in 1837. It is much smaller than his former plate, engraved in 1827, and not as good. It has a fac-simile of Shakespeare's autograph underneath it.

Campbell's Shakespeare, London: 1838, 8vo., has a copy from Houbraken's plate, engraved by H. Robinson, which is not satisfactory.

The second edition of Wivell's *Inquiry*, London: 1840, 8vo., contained a plate by B. Holl, from Houbraken's print, in which the countenance is made much whiter than in the original. The same plate was used in Stebbing's Shakespeare, London: (1845–51. ?) Another engraving of this, much smaller, and in an oval, by Holl, is quite fair. *Circa* 1845.

In *Religious and Moral Sentences Culled from the*

Works of Shakespeare, etc., London: 1847, is the smallest engraving from the Chandos portrait ever published. It is about half an inch in diameter, and engraved on wood.

B. Holl again copied Houbraken's print *circa* 1850; and E. Scriven also about the same time engraved a plate from the original painting, which was published by Charles Knight, and is quite a good representation of it.

The "Select Portrait Gallery" in the *Guide to Knowledge*, *circa* 1850, contained an engraving from Humphry's drawing, fairly done, but with head reversed, and figure added from the original painting and somewhat altered.

In 1849 Samuel Cousins engraved a magnificent mezzotint for the old Shakespeare Society, which is by far the finest copy ever made of this portrait. Seen in an artist's proof it is very fine. It represents the portrait as if in perfect condition, and none of the defects wrought by time and injudicious cleaning appear in this engraving. A good photograph of this print was published in Friswell's *Life Portraits*, etc., London: 1864, 8vo.

About this date S. Freeman engraved a copy of Humphry's drawing, which is quite good, but has the head and figure reversed.

Tallis' Shakespeare, London: (1851?,) 4to., contains a fair engraving by Hollis. It is surrounded by portraits of Queen Elizabeth, Queen Victoria, Mr. Macready, and Mrs. Warner.

A very poor copy, on wood, by G. Dalziel, was published in Knight's Cabinet edition of Shakespeare, in 1851.

The same year T. D. Scott made a very unsatisfactory copy from Humphry's drawing, which was engraved by G. Greatbach (*Circa* 1851).

About this time T. H. Ellis published a large and very curious plate, but the names of the copyist and engraver are not given. It is from the Chandos portrait, but the head is lengthened, the nose made much longer, the beard so drawn as to make the chin look longer, and the whole expression of the face much altered. The figure is turned more in profile, the shoulders represented as too sloping, and no attempt has been made to give the stone arch surrounding the portrait in the original.

Hudson's first edition of Shakespeare, Boston: 1856, 16mo., contains a wretched copy of the Chandos portrait.

John Faed, F.S.A., painted a large picture of Shakespeare, using the Chandos portrait for the head, which he has idealized very much. The poet is represented seated at a table, with his pen in one hand, and his head resting on the other. A book-case in the rear, with books piled on the floor, another chair, and an elegant curtain, form the other accessories of the picture, and represent a style of magnificence which Shakespeare certainly never enjoyed, unless Mr. Faed meant to represent him writing in the house of one of his noble patrons. James Faed engraved a large plate from this painting, which was published in 1859 by Henry Graves & Co.

Staunton's *Memorials of Shakespeare*, London: 1864, folio, has a very good photograph of the Chandos by Preston.

A beautiful lithograph, by P. Rohrbach, from a drawing by Hermann Berg, and published by E. H. Schroeder, Berlin, in 1864, is worthy of all praise, both for its accuracy and softness.

A chromo-lithograph, by Frank Jones, and published in 1872, by Bencke and Jones, New York, is the size of the original, and possesses some merit.

A very good copy of Cousins' mezzotint, engraved by R. A. Artlett, was published by Vertue & Co., in their Imperial edition of Knight's Shakespeare, London: 1875, folio.

The Death Mask.

FROM PHOTOGRAPH OF ORIGINAL BY PAGE.

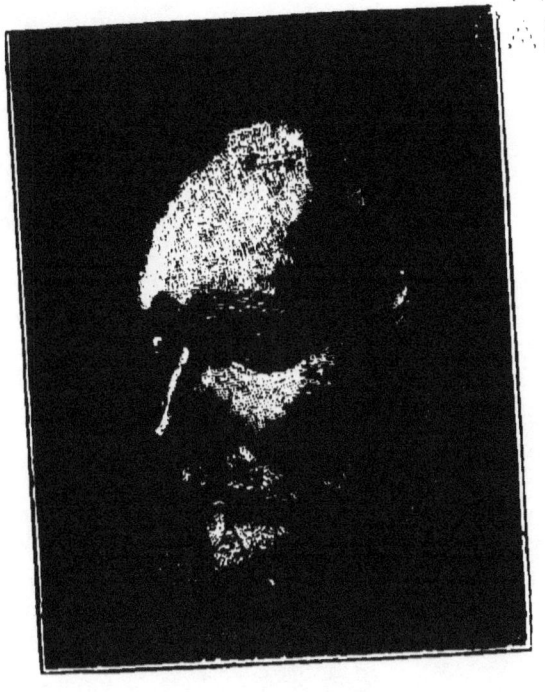

UNIV. OF
CALIFORNIA

THE DEATH MASK.

ON November 18, 1841, Count and Canon Francis von Kesselstadt died in Mayence, or, more properly Mainz. He was the only surviving heir of an old and noble family which had lived in Cologne for many years. He had inherited many pictures, and had himself added to the collection which descended to him from his ancestors. Among these were portraits of many historical personages, including those of Albrecht von Brandenburg, Gustavus Adolphus, Henry IV., Martin Luther, Melanchthon, Albrecht Dürer, and Martin Schön. He also had a number of portraits of celebrated poets, and, among the latter, was a small picture painted in oil, on parchment, representing the corpse of a man, crowned with a wreath, lying in state on a bed. In the background is a burning taper, faintly represented, and the date, in gilt, Aō 1637.

This picture is said to have been in the possession

of the Kesselstadt family at Cologne, for more than a century, and Professor Müller, the Director of the Picture Gallery in Mayence, who knew the Count and Canon Francis Von Kesselstadt quite well from the year 1790, said that he had seen it in the Count's collection. He stated further that it occupied a prominent place in that nobleman's residence, and that it bore the inscription:

"Traditionen nach Shakespeare."*

Professor Müller also said that he knew the Count refused "some very handsome offers from parties anxious to become purchasers" of it, and that it was always received by all the visitors to his gallery as an authentic portrait of Shakespeare.

In June, 1842, the Count's pictures, etc., were sold at auction, in Mayence, and this little painting was purchased by S. Jourdan, an antiquary living in that town. In 1845 or 1846 Ludwig Becker moved to Mayence, where he saw the picture in Jourdan's possession, and finally bought it from him in 1847.

Becker was a portrait painter by profession, and originally resided in Darmstadt. The Grand Duke of

---

* "According to tradition, Shakespeare."

The Death Mask.

From Photograph of Original by Page.

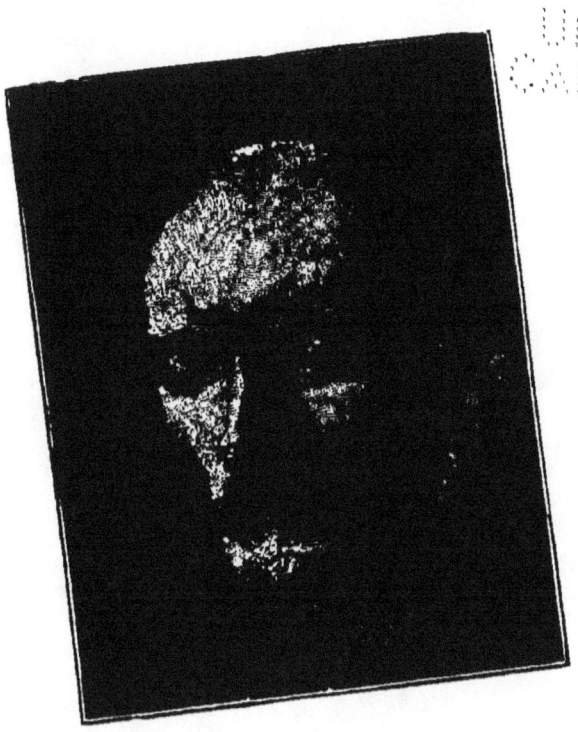

UNIV. OF
CALIFORNIA

Hesse appointed him "Court Painter," and his miniatures in water colors were much valued.

In this connection it is only proper to state that Ludwig Becker, in a little pamphlet in which he gives the details of his purchase, etc., of this portrait, says that Count and Canon Francis von Kesselstadt died in the year 1843; but the date given above as the year of his death (1841) is that stated by Dr. Hermann Schaaffhausen in his article "Ueber die Todtenmaske Shakespeare's," published in the *Jahrbuch* of the German Shakespeare Society for 1875. Dr. Schaaffhausen further states that the picture is 2 inches 4 lines (Rhenish measure) high, and 3 inches 8 lines wide; and that the entry in the sale catalogue of the Kesselstadt pictures, etc., is as follows: "A Deceased, with laurel-crowned head, 1637."

The date on the picture, 1637, did not correspond with the year in which Shakespeare died (1616), and Becker conceived the idea that it had probably been copied from some older one or from a cast or statue. He subsequently ascertained that a plaster of Paris cast of a face had also formed part of the Count's collection, but that on the sale of his effects it had received little consideration, and no one remembered who had bought it. Becker was not discouraged, however, and in 1849, two years after he had purchased the little picture, he tells us that he found the Mask he was searching for in Mayence, "in a broker's shop, amongst rags and articles of the meanest description."

Becker states that he at once recognized the Mask from its likeness to the picture, and adds that "by adorning the cast with a wreath of cypress, and adding the same colored hair as in the picture, the pale chiselled features will assuredly awaken the endless respect which his works have gained for him."

At the risk of repeating what has been said above, it has been thought desirable to give, in a translation, the following little pamphlet issued by Becker, and referred to above:

"In the year 1843, the Count and Canon Francis von Kesselstadt died at Mayence. In the same year his valuable collection of curiosities and objects of art was disposed of by auction. Amongst other things, there was an unornamented small-sized oil painting (the picture of a corpse,) which an antiquary of the town of Mayence bought at the sale. In the year 1847, I gained possession of it by purchase (see the documents herewith.) Professor Müller, of Mayence, knew the history of this picture, and communicated it to me by letter. In the mean time I happened to see another oil painting,

The Death Mask.

FROM PHOTOGRAPHS OF ORIGINAL.

which, being amongst his most valued pictures, was hung in his own bed room, being considered to be a portrait of Shakespeare. It was painted in oil on parchment, and bore the date 1637. As this date does not coincide with the date of Shakespeare's death, 1616, I stated my opinion to brother antiquarians that this picture must, in all probability, be copied from an older one, or possibly have been arrived at from some existing cast or statue. I then learned that in this same collection of Graf Kesselstadt, there had been a plaster of Paris cast, which, on account of its melancholy appearance, had been treated with little consideration; who had bought it, nobody knew. After two years' fruitless search and inquiry, in the year 1849 I discovered the lost relic in a broker's shop, amongst rags and articles of the meanest description.

"The back of it bears the inscription—

† A^o D^o_m 1616.

"On carefully comparing the cast with the picture, I could no longer doubt that the pair were to be identified as of the same person.

"By adorning the cast with a wreath of cypress, and adding the same colored hair as in the picture, the pale chiselled features will assuredly awaken the endless respect which his works have gained for him.

"LUDWIG BECKER."

"Edinburgh, 1850."

TRANSLATION

OF

MÜLLER'S LETTER TO L. BECKER.

———

"Mayence, 28th February, 1847.

"FRIEND BECKER:

"Some time ago you submitted for my opinion a small oil painting—a sort of miniature in oils—of the English school, painted in the seventeenth century. This picture represented a very celebrated Englishman, lying on his death-bed, in state. I remarked at the time, that in the features of the deceased, I instantly recognized those of that great European dramatic author, William Shakespeare, of Stratford, born in 1564, and on his death-bed, alas! in 1616. You now request me to state, by letter, my reasons for the above opinion, it being of importance just now that you should know them.

"I have not the least hesitation in communicating the following:

The Kesselstadt Picture.

From Photograph of Original.

"The picture in question was upwards of a century in the hands of the noble family of Kesselstadt, at Cologne; which city, it is well known, kept up a lively commerce in works of art with London, for nearly three hundred years. The deceased Prebendary,* Francis Earl of Kesselstadt (with whom I was on terms of intimacy since the year 1790,) as only surviving heir, succeeded to the estates, and became possessed of all the pictures and *chef-d'œuvres*. He himself had considerable knowledge of painting; was a great collector, as well as a lover and patron of the Fine Arts. He turned his attention, however, more particularly to works of historical worth, the portraits of renowned characters, of which he had a large collection, and to each of which he appended a sort of historical reference, *par exemple*, Albrecht von Brandenburg, Gustavus Adolphus (King of Sweden), Henry IV., Martin Luther, Melanchthon, Albrecht Durer, Martin Schön; and, amongst the celebrated poets of the olden time, the little picture now in your possession had a prominent place, bearing the inscription,—

'TRADITIONEN NACH SHAKESPEARE.'

This picture came into your possession after the death

---

* Domherr.

of Earl Kesselstadt, when his effects were put up at auction; and thus you had the opportunity and good fortune of acquiring, at a moderate price, a gem of art and 'world-celebrated rarity.' I cannot here omit stating, that among all the numerous *savans*, antiquaries, and eminent artists visiting Earl Kesselstadt's gallery, not the least doubt existed as to the authenticity of the picture of Shakespeare, to which many affirmed the sketches they had seen in England bore strong resemblance.

"Earl Kesselstadt, to my knowledge, refused some very handsome offers from parties anxious to become purchasers.

"Your friend,

"(Signed)   N. MÜLLER,

"*Professor*."

"In testimony of the authenticity of Professor Müller's signature.

"(Signed)   NACK,

"*Burgomaster of Mayence*."

"Mayence, 28th February, 1847."

Translation of
Certificate of Purchase from
S. Jourdan, an Antiquary of Mayence.

"17th March, 1847.

"I hereby certify, at the request of Mr. L. Becker, that the little picture, bearing date 1637, and representing Shakespeare upon his death-bed, was purchased by me at the public sale of Earl Kesselstadt's effects, and afterwards sold to the above Mr. L. Becker.

"(Signed) S. Jourdan,
"Antiquary, Mayence."

"In testimony of the authenticity of S. Jourdan's signature.

"(Signed) Nack,
"Burgomaster of Mayence."

"Mayence, 17th March, 1847."

Some critics (Friswell among the number,) have agreed with Becker, that the picture is a copy from the Mask, but others cannot see any resemblance between the two. Among the latter class the present writer begs to enrol himself.

The features which are shown in the little oil painting bear a far greater resemblance to those of Ben Jonson than to Shakespeare. Indeed, the resemblance to the picture of Ben Jonson in the Dulwich Gallery is quite striking. The inscription on the painting, 1637, is also the year that Ben Jonson died, and if the latter represents him lying in state, then the date is correct. To suppose, however, that the figures refer to the year that the picture was painted, if it be taken as a portrait of Shakespeare, is a much more difficult matter. No artist making a copy of a man's face who had died in 1616, would put the date that he made the copy (1637) in such a prominent place.

How can the fact of a Mask of Shakespeare being in the collection of a German nobleman, long after the poet's death, be explained?

Two theories have been suggested. One, that an ancestor of Count and Canon Francis von Kesselstadt had been in England, and bought the Mask while there, as a relic of the great poet; and the other that Gerard Johnson's sons returned to their father's native city of Amsterdam, and brought the Mask with them; which they, or their father, had used in making the Stratford bust. The latter conjecture is that of Karl Elze, and seems much more probable than the former; for no member of the Kesselstadt family is known to have gone to England, though of course some one of them might have done so without any record of his journey having been preserved.

If Gerard Johnson, or his sons, had a mask, taken from the face of Shakespeare after death, for their use in making the Stratford bust (and some of the best judges have declared that that effigy was sculptured from a mask,) certainly there is no improbability in the sons of Johnson taking the cast with them, after it had served its purpose, when they returned to Amsterdam.

If we advance one step further, and are willing to admit that this was the Mask which was so used by Gerard Johnson or his sons, and that it had been thus brought to Amsterdam, it will be easy to believe that it could have found its way from thence to Cologne, where the Kesselstadts formerly lived; and that it could have been bought by some member of that family.

Here occurs, however, a very serious break in the chain of argument. How do we know that this Mask was ever in the Count's collection? It is true that Becker states that he "learned that, in this same collection of Graf Kesselstadt, there had been a plaster of Paris cast, which, on account of its melancholy appearance, had been treated with little consideration; who had bought it nobody knew." But Becker does not tell us how he got this information, and there is no further proof forthcoming; nor does Prof. Müller mention the Mask in his letter to Becker.

The theories which have been advanced to explain the possession of the Mask by Count and Canon Francis von Kesselstadt, have been before referred to, but how is the picture of the man on his death-bed to be accounted for? If this really be a picture of Ben Jonson, as it is believed to be by some, Professor Müller may have confounded the picture with the Mask, and it may have been the latter which had "According to tradition, Shakespeare," under it, in the Count's collection. Perhaps, however, "'twere to consider too curiously, to consider so."

The Mask has evidently been made from a dead face. It is of plaster of Paris, and of a dirty yellow color. This yellowish appearance is owing to the oil with which it has been covered, and which has soaked into it. The oil was probably rubbed on it when another copy was made from it, and would seem to indicate that it has been used to model from. Some hairs adhere to the moustache and the beard on the Mask, and also on the eyebrows and eyelashes. These hairs have been proven, by examination with the microscope, to be human. They are of a reddish brown or auburn color, and correspond to the color of the beard and hair of the Stratford bust, and the description of its original color on that effigy. With regard to this, however, it is only proper to state that the hair of a person which has been naturally of a dark color when living, often turns to a reddish brown on being cut off and kept for a long time. This is probably caused by chemical change in the coloring matter of the hair, owing to want of the nourishment which it received when growing.

To explain how these hairs became affixed to the Mask, it will be necessary to say a few words about the manner in which masks are made, which was probably followed in making this one also. The first process is to make an impression or mould of the face. A band of cloth is placed around the head of the person whose face is to be copied. This band encircles the head about where the ears are, and leaves exposed all the chin and forehead—in fact, the entire face in front of it. Soft wax is then poured over the face, and is kept by the band from running too far. It quickly hardens, and is easily removed. The eyebrows, eyelashes, moustache, and beard have been previously greased, or covered with soap and water, to prevent the wax from adhering to the hairs. In spite of this precaution, however, some few of the hairs will adhere to the mould, and are pulled out of the skin when the wax is removed. This mould is now an exact copy of the face from which it has been taken, but, of course, it is the opposite of a human face, for where the protuberances of the latter are, they are represented in the mould by corresponding indentations. Among sculptors the result of this process is known as a "flying mould."

The mould is then oiled and filled with liquid plaster of Paris or wax. When this is taken out of the mould, a perfect cast representing each detail of the face from which it was taken appears, and in this process some of the hairs which had adhered to the mould are transferred to the cast. Frequently the mould becomes broken in making a cast, and then the cast has to be oiled to make another mould. The yellowish appearance of the Death Mask would indicate, as before stated, that it had been used in this way. A cast of the face only is technically termed a "mask."

It would seem probable in the case of the Death Mask that a wax mask was first cast in the mould, as the Mask shows a slight wave along the bridge of the nose, and also a flattened surface, where the pores of the skin—which are everywhere else perceptible—are lost. This has been caused by some pressure on the nose. Had it been exerted on the dead face, the structure of the nasal organ would have resisted the pressure, and no such flatness would have resulted as appears in the Death Mask. From this wax face another mould was probably made, and in this the Death Mask was cast.

Now let us trace the course that the hairs adhering to the Death Mask would have to take if this theory be correct. From the dead face they adhered to the wax "flying mould." In this was cast a wax face, and they adhered to this; and from this cast another mould was made, either of wax or plaster, which retained the hairs. In this mould the Death Mask was finally cast, and these hairs appear in it. The hairs could easily pass from one to the other—from mould to mask, and *vice versa*—as no precautions were probably taken to prevent them from doing so.

The Death Mask is in a fair state of preservation. A small fragment has been broken off the lower right side of the nose. Some persons have thought that this was caused by a portion of the plaster having there adhered to the mould; but the shape of the damaged place is such as to lead to the conclusion that it was the result of a blow from the side. On the other side of the nose there are indications of the plaster having been touched with a knife. Lines have been cut in the moustache and goatee to represent the hairs. A portion of the left upper lip has been accidentally removed, and a part of the eyelashes of the left eye have disappeared.

Over the right eyebrow there is an indentation or scar on the forehead of the Mask extending towards the right side. More will be said about this hereafter.

On the back edge of the Mask there has been placed the inscription:

† A^{o} D$\overline{\text{m}}$ 1616.

It has evidently been made with a blunt stick when the plaster was soft, and has no appearance of having been cut afterwards. If the latter had been the case, the letters would have presented a sharper appearance than they do. The figures are similar to those used at the date inscribed on it, and there is no reason to suppose that they were put there at a later date. The cross which precedes them is often met with in inscriptions on tomb stones, etc., and the "A^{o} D$\overline{\text{m}}$" is an abbreviation for "Anno Domini."

The same inscription is also to be seen on two other angles in the interior of the Mask. Here they have not been touched by persons handling the cast, and they are in a better state of preservation than those first referred to, which are more exposed.

The surface of the Mask represents the pores of the skin with the greatest accuracy, and the incised lines which appear in the moustache and goatee are those which have been made by the person making the Mask. It is impossible to obtain a cast of each hair as in life, for the grease and plaster cause them to stick together, and it is usual to cut lines in the cast to imitate the hair. This must not be supposed to detract from the evidence that it is a cast from a face, and it furnishes no argument in favor of the Mask being a mere work of art. Indeed the surface of the skin so perfectly exhibited in the Mask forbids any such idea.

Regarding the question whether the art of making masks was known as early as Shakespeare's time, it can safely be answered in the affirmative. Long before the time of Pliny (A. D. 23) they were made. In his *Historia Naturalis*, published about A. D. 77, he states that the first person who made a plaster mould of a human face, from which a cast was subsequently made, was Lysistratus of Sicyon (B. C. 321). It is true that Pliny does not state that the mould was taken from a dead face; but if they were able to take them from the living, it would be easier to make a mould from the dead.

The passage in Pliny's *Historia Naturalis*, Lib. XXXV, 44, is as follows:

"Hominis autem imaginem gypso e facie ipsa primus omnium expressit, ceraque in eam formam gypsi infusa emendare instituit Lysistratus Sicyonius, frater Lysippi, de quo diximus. Hic et similitudinem reddere instituit: ante eum quam pulcherrimas facere studebant. Idem et de signis effigiem exprimere invenit. Crevitque res in tantum, ut nulla signa, statuæve, sine argilla fierent. Quo apparet, antiquiorem hanc fuisse scientiam, quam fundendi aeris."

A mask of Martin Luther is in existence. He died at Eisleben in 1546. Another one of Tasso, who died in 1595, is also extant.

It has been suggested that many of the figures in the old monuments in existence in England have probably been modelled from casts made from moulds taken from the faces of those that they represent, and their placid expression would seem to support this theory. If this be so there must have been men in England who understood how to make a mould from a dead face. Wax was, also, often used, and casts of the faces of celebrated persons were frequently colored and used on lay figures. These were dressed in the garments worn by the deceased in life, and doubtless many who saw them lying in state believed them to be the actual bodies. In the Chapel of St. Erasmus, Westminster Abbey, in an old closet, many of these lay figures may still be seen. In an account of the Abbey, published in 1754, it is stated that "these effigies resembled the deceased as nearly as possible, and were wont to be exposed at the funerals of our princes, and other great personages, in open chariots, with their proper ensigns of royalty or honor appended." The same account states that the effigy of King Edward VI., was originally clothed in crimson velvet robes, but time had made these resemble leather; but that those of Queen Elizabeth and King James I. were stripped of everything of value. The effigies of King William, Queen Mary, and Queen Anne were handsomely dressed in lace and velvet. Here, also, were the figures of Nelson and Cromwell.

Dr. Schaaffhausen says: "The custom of erecting an effigy of the deceased, made from the corpse, appears to be a very old one. Indeed the coffins of the Egyptian mummies represent a human figure. The British Museum possesses a face mask made of gold plate, said to be that of Nebuchadnezzar.

"The custom, which was practiced in Egypt of gilding the faces of mummies of distinguished persons, is perhaps the origin of such modelling. Carus represents in his *Atlas der Cranioscopie* (Taf. XXIII) the mummy of an old Egyptian king or priest of Memphis, whose head, hands, and feet were gilded.

"In Christian churches skulls of saints, in portrait-busts

of burnished silver, were often preserved, the head of which enclosed the skull like a case. In the Golden Chamber of the Ursula Church, at Cologne, there are several of these portrait-busts." *

In 1849 Ludwig Becker went to England, taking the Mask and the little oil painting with him. Here they were examined by the authorities of the British Museum and by many others. In 1850 Becker went to Melbourne, leaving the Mask and picture in the custody of Professor Owen, of the British Museum. While in the latter gentleman's possession they were seen by many persons, and in 1864 they were exhibited at Stratford-upon-Avon, at the Tercentenary celebration of Shakespeare's birthday.

Becker died April 24, 1861, while on an expedition across the Australian continent under the auspices of the British Government. On the fact of his death becoming known to Professor Owen, the latter returned the Mask and picture to his brothers, and since then they have been in the custody of Dr. Ernest Becker, the curator of the Grand Ducal Museum at Darmstadt.

Professor Owen, of the British Museum, stated that if the fact that the Mask originally came from England

---

* Translated from *Ueber die Todtenmaske Shakespeare's* in the *Jahrbuch* of the German Shakespeare Society, Vol. X. Weimar: 1875, 8vo., p. 28.

could be satisfactorily established, there was hardly any price that the Museum would have hesitated to pay for it. It is said that ten thousand pounds was the sum Becker asked for it.

Regarding the indentation over the right eyebrow, which has been referred to above, Professor John S. Hart, who saw the Mask in Darmstadt, wrote that it was "merely a flake of the plaster fallen or rubbed off." William Page subsequently went to Darmstadt specially to examine the Death Mask. He says, concerning this indentation: "From the photographs, I knew there must be some indentation and a loss of the texture of the skin in this discolored place, which, for some reason, had received the colored wash thus unequally.

"My first attempt to take an impression of this spot, together with a part of the forehead, failed, having tried it in soft modelling wax, which adhered somewhat, and was distorted and lost in removing; but the *depression* in the spot was well shown in the *relief* of the wax at that point. My next attempt was in white, harder wax, with gauze intervening. This mould, though less delicate in parts, was very successful, and gave me a good cast in plaster; where the *indentation* is plainly visible, it may, perhaps, have been looked on as a defect, and has certainly been partially filled up. In the plain white of plaster the depression is still to be seen, though in the discolored spot over the brow I could not at first detect it." *

Mr. Page also made a number of measures from the Death Mask, which he afterwards compared with the Stratford bust. Concerning these he says: "Of these twenty-six measures, at least ten or twelve fit exactly corresponding points in the Stratford bust, which any one may verify, if he will take the trouble to interpret the diagram here annexed, and reduce all the measurements to solid geometry. Few persons need be told that this planet never did, at any one moment, contain two adult heads, whose faces agreed in any dozen like measures, and the law of probabilities makes it remote when such an epoch will arrive. To a working artist's mind, the agreement of these measures is either a miracle, or demonstration that they are from the same face.

"And, still further, the failure or misfit of the other more than dozen measures is confined to those parts of the face where there is acknowledged error on the part of the sculptor of the Stratford bust. In the language of science, 'measures are the inflexible judges placed above all opinions supported only by imperfect observations.'

---

* *A Study of Shakespeare's Portraits.* London: 1876, 48mo., p. 59.

"It is, indeed, singular that such an agreement in measure with the Stratford bust should not have been noted or published by the distinguished scholars and scientists in whose care the Mask was during its sojourn in England; but so far as I know, it has not hitherto been done." *

Friswell thought that the appearance of the left eye of the mask indicated "that the process of decay had set in before the cast was taken, part of the cornea protruding from beneath the eyelid. This is the case with the same eye, and, curiously, with the mask of Cromwell's face." †

Whereupon Page says: "I shall refer to only one more accidental break, and that of slight importance, except in its misconstruction; it is where a part of the massing of the eyelashes in the left eye has been broken off. It has been cited and repeated, that here, as in the same eye in the mask of Cromwell, decay had set in, and something ran out. * * * * * The error in regard to the eye has arisen probably from forgetting or not knowing that it is usual to mass the hairs of the eyelashes, brows, and beard with soap or paste, or some such preparation, to prevent the substance of the mould from pulling out or sticking to these hairs. I have never seen a more healthy cast

---

* *A Study of Shakespeare's Portraits.* London: 1876, 48mo., p. 48.
† *Life Portraits*, etc. London: 1864, 8vo., p. 17.

from a dead face; and if Shakespeare was buried at Stratford, in April, two days after his death,* there certainly was no time for decay in his eyes; and the rest of his face shows the most natural and perfect condition, as though he might have fallen asleep in perfect health. If this mask is from Shakespeare, his illness must have been short, producing the least possible apparent change of his countenance; and the most fortunate moment afterwards was chosen for casting the face." †

Friswell thus compares the Death Mask and the Stratford bust: "The Mask has a short upper lip, the bust a very long one; but this discrepancy is accounted for on the supposition that the sculptor had an accident with the nose. The nostrils are drawn up, almost painfully; the same is visible in the bust. There are several other points of resemblance, but these are very minute.

"On the other hand, the cast differs very widely from the bust *said* to have been cut from it. The nose is utterly unlike; in the cast it is a fine, thin, aquiline nose, and, as there can be no doubt that the cast is from a dead face, one feels irresistibly the force of Mrs. Quickly's *simile* in the much-contested quotation, as altered by Mr. Collier's 'old corrector;'

---

* Shakespeare died April 23, 1616, and was buried on the 25th of the same month.
† *A Study of Shakespeare's Portraits.* London: 1876, 48mo., p. 57.

" 'His nose was as sharp as a pen on a table of green frieze.'

"The face is a sharp oval, that of the bust is a blunt one; the chin is narrow and pointed, that of the bust rounded or rather square, and full of force; the cheeks are thin and drawn in, those of the bust full, fat, and almost coarse. Exception has also been taken to the age of the person expressed in this cast, some asserting that it is too young in look for the years of our poet at his death. But here we are in favor of the cast. Some time after death the skin seems to relax, the wrinkles to fill out, and the expression of care becomes one of quietude and peace. There are, moreover, plenty of indications of 'crow's feet' and wrinkles at the corners of the eyes; and the face, while it wants utterly the jovial look of the bust, is certainly one of a person who might have suffered, thought, and felt. * * * * * *

"Lastly, it may be noted in regard to the Mask of the face in the custody of Professor Owen, that the extreme thinness of the nose and of the cheeks does not so much militate against its genuineness as one would suppose. The features alter extremely after death with most persons; and although Shakespeare is said to have died after a very short illness, he may have lost much flesh. The 'tombe maker,' wishing to exhibit him *ad vivum*, would alter this. As a parallel instance of extreme difference between life and death, we may cite the cast from the features of Napoleon the Great preserved in the Invalides. Looking at it, with its drawn face and sharpened nose, one would rather think it a mask of the fine, thin features of Voltaire, than of the round and massive head of the conqueror Napoleon I." *

Some years ago W. J. Thoms suggested that the Death Mask might be that of Cervantes, the author of *Don Quixote*, who died in Madrid in 1616. He further added that the features of the Mask resembled the pictures of Cervantes more than Shakespeare.

The portraits of Cervantes which are extant are all founded on a description of his appearance given by the author of *Don Quixote* himself. He describes himself as having a long face, chestnut-brown hair, silver-gray beard, which was originally of a golden color; a smooth, open brow, a clear eye with animated expression, a well-formed, aquiline nose, very small mouth, defective teeth, a light complexion, and medium height. From this description artists have constructed portraits of Cervantes, but no picture or engraving of him has any other authority for its foundation.

Cervantes died in the greatest poverty and his burial

---

* *Life Portraits*, etc. London: 1864, 8vo., pp. 17, 26.

was of the plainest description. No ceremony of any kind is known to have been observed, and no tombstone was erected over his grave. In view of such facts as these, is it at all probable that any one should have conceived the idea of making a mask from his face?

Another fact in relation to this matter remains to be stated. Cervantes was born in 1547 and did not die until 1616. He was therefore sixty-nine years old at the time of his death. The latter was caused by dropsy. Now the Death Mask resembles the face of a man of fifty-two, which was Shakespeare's age, much more nearly than sixty-nine, and no one for an instant will think that it has any resemblance to the face of one who died of dropsy—where the features are much swollen.

Mr. Page always had the greatest faith in the Death Mask. He desired to paint a portrait of Shakespeare, and decided to adopt the Mask as the basis of his work, using also the Stratford bust, the Droeshout engraving, and the Chandos portrait. He first obtained thirteen photographs representing the Mask from different points of view. From these he made two clay masks of life size, but finally he decided to make a colossal mask in plaster.

This he did, and in another one of similar size he restored the small portions missing in the original Death Mask. In August, 1874, he went to Darmstadt specially to see the Mask. Dr. Becker gave him the fullest facilities for examining it, and permitted him to take photographs of it, to make accurate measurements with calipers, and impressions from portions of it. On his return to New York he made a life-sized bust in plaster, from which a bronze casting was finally obtained.

This bust is very handsome, and is a faithful rendering of the Mask. It is of the head and shoulders only. Looking at it from the front, one sees how strong the likeness is to the Stratford bust. The opening of the eyes by Mr. Page, and giving the face an air of life, instead of the painfully sad expression shown in the Death Mask, of course has much to do with this; but let any unprejudiced and competent critic place this bust alongside of a gray cast of the Stratford one, and he will be struck with the resemblance between them. The chief points of difference are the short nose of the Stratford bust as compared with the longer one of Page's bust, and the more receding forehead of the latter in opposition to the prominent one of the Stratford bust.

A beautiful crayon drawing of Page's bust, representing the full-face view, was made, it is believed, by the artist himself, and the few photographs of this which were taken are treasured by their fortunate possessors. Numerous photographs of this bust have also been taken by Sarony, some of which do not do it justice.

Mr. Page also painted a three-quarter length portrait from the Death Mask, which has met with some unfavorable criticism, and which is certainly not as fine as his bust. The poet is represented as having risen from a chair, and is standing by a table, on which he rests his left hand. In his right hand he holds a book, and is looking down as if in thought. This shows the eyelids drooping, and gives the face a somewhat sleepy expression. A large photograph from this picture, by W. Kurtz, was published in 1875 by Louis Menger, New York.

J. Niessen drew a crayon portrait of the Death Mask, bringing it to life as Page did, but, unlike the latter, he confined himself to the Mask alone. Niessen's drawing exhibits a three-quarter face, and has a very animated expression. Its chief fault is in the too great prominence of the chin. Several excellent photographs of it have been published, and some of the larger ones are strikingly handsome.

Of the Death Mask itself numerous photographs have been taken, representing it in many positions. The best are those by Page.

THE JANSEN PORTRAIT.

THE history of this beautiful picture is very unsatisfactory, and the little that is known concerning it does not establish the fact that it is an authentic portrait of Shakespeare.

In the first place, it is not known who painted it. It is generally called the Jansen portrait (though frequently known as "the Somerset") and is supposed to have been painted by Cornelius Jansen. The latter's name is also spelled Janssen or Janssens, and sometimes Johnson— although the latter is incorrect.

This celebrated painter was born in Amsterdam in 1590. The exact date when he came to England is not known, but the first paintings there that can with certainty be ascribed to him are dated about 1618. This is two years after Shakespeare died, and to establish the fact of this portrait having been painted from life by Jansen (if it really be a portrait of Shakespeare), it must be

The Jansen Portrait.

FROM MEZZOTINT BY CHARLES TURNER.

By Hanoch Mccutcht.

proven that the painter came to England in 1610, or prior to that year, for the picture bears that date. With the present knowledge of Jansen's history this cannot be done. It is true that Sandrart said he was born in London, and that his parents were Flemish,* but Walpole (in his *Anecdotes of Painting*) does not credit this statement, while Vertue, and the author of *An Essay Towards an English School*, give Amsterdam as the place of his birth. Mr. Ralph N. Wornum in his edition of Walpole's *Anecdotes of Painting* (London: 1849, 8vo., Vol. I, p. 211,) cites Immerzeel, *Levens en Werken der Hollandsche Kunstschilders* as additional authority for the fact of Jansen having been born in Amsterdam; and he allows Walpole's assertion that "Jansen's first works in England are dated about 1618" to pass without comment. This, in a profusely annotated and carefully edited book like Wor-

---

* The passage from Sandrart, *Academiæ Picturæ Nobilis*, Caput xx, p. 314, is as follows:

"232. Cornelius Jansonius Londinensis.

"Belgis propterea annumerari potest, quia Parentes ejus in Belgico Hispanico nati fuerant, et ob tumultus saltem bellicos Londinum concesserant, ubi hunc deinde genuere filium. Hic cum ad artem pictoriam sese applicuisset, iconibus potissimum conficiendis operam dedit; unde in servitia Caroli Stuarti Regis Angliæ assumtus, Regis atque Reginæ, totiusque aulæ elegantes elaborabat effigies. Ortis autem inter Regem hunc atque Parlamentum dissidiis, adeoque in turbas hasce involutâ totâ Anglia, Jansonius noster una fere cum omnibus celebri oribus artificibus aliis ex Anglia discedebat, translato in Hollandiam tum temporis omni felicitatis genere affluentem, domicilio; ibidemque postquam icones confecisset egregias plurimas, tandem anno 1665. Amstelodami ex hac miseriarum valle emigravit."

num's, must be taken as an endorsement of what his author has said.

Walpole further states that Jansen took up his residence in Blackfriars, London, had much business, and his price "for a head was five broad pieces." Walpole also asserts that "at Sherburn Castle, in Dorsetshire, is a head of Elizabeth Wriothesley, eldest daughter of Henry, Earl of Southampton, and wife of William, Lord Spencer," which is by Jansen. At Charlecote Hall, Warwickshire, formerly the residence of Sir Thomas Lucy, there is a large painting of Sir Thomas' family, including his wife and six children, which is also said to have been painted by Jansen. Dallaway gives a list of thirty-two portraits, which he considers were certainly Jansen's work during his stay in England, and says that there are many others, which are claimed to be by him, which closely resemble his style. Dallaway states that Jansen copied portraits of the ancestors of several of the nobility, "in the possession of others, and those have borne his name, which the comparative dates would not otherwise warrant."

In 1648 he left England and returned to Amsterdam, after first going to Midelburg. He died in Amsterdam in 1665.

If Jansen really did come to England early enough to

have painted this portrait of Shakespeare in 1610, he must then have been only twenty years old, for it will be remembered that he was born in 1590. None of the portraits mentioned by Walpole as having been painted by Jansen in England are dated this early. Walpole's words are: "Jansen's first works in England are dated about 1618." This alleged portrait of Shakespeare is not mentioned by Walpole, nor is it given in the undoubted works by Jansen recorded by Dallaway, and above referred to. Still the picture bears a strong resemblance in its manner and general treatment to undoubted works of Jansen. It has the same dark background that is so often found in his pictures, and its neat, clear, and smooth appearance agrees with Jansen's style.

It is only proper that an assertion of Malone's should be here noticed. In his *Life of Shakespeare* (edition of 1821, Vol. II, page 429,) he notices Walpole's statement with regard to the date of Jansen's arrival in England, and states that he (Malone) has a portrait painted by that artist, dated 1611, "which had belonged for more than a century to a family that lived at Chelsea." But Malone does not give his authority for stating that it is a portrait by Jansen, nor any further information concerning it. Had he told us who his portrait represented, it could have been identified, whereas now his statement has comparatively little value. It might have been a portrait by Jansen not painted in England.

Charles Jennens published an edition of *King Lear* in 1770. This was the first time that any editor of Shakespeare gave the various readings of the old Quartos and Folios on the same page as the text. Capell had previously made extensive collations, which were published separately from his edition (*Notes and Various Readings*, 1779–81), but Jennens first printed the collations on the same page with the text.

Jennens' name did not appear on the title-page. Indeed, he did all he could to mislead the reader as to the editorship of the volume, as he dedicated it to himself, spoke of the patronage extended to the editor by Mr. Jennens, and acknowledged the editor's indebtedness to that gentleman for access to books in his library. But the part of this edition of *King Lear* which concerns the subject of the present essay is the fact that it contained a soft and beautiful mezzotint by R. Earlom. Under it appeared the inscription: "William Shakespear. From an Original Picture by Cornelius Jansen in the Collection of C. Jennens Esqr.;" and in the left corner: "*R. Earlom fecit.*"

Jennens' house was at Gopsal, Leicestershire, and the publication of this engraving of the Jansen portrait was the first public announcement that such a picture was in existence. Neither Jennens nor any one else ever published any account of where the picture came from, or how he obtained it.

The Critical Review for December, 1770, contained a notice of Jennens' edition of *King Lear*, which is supposed to have been written by Steevens. In it Earlom's mezzotint is thus referred to:

"*King Lear*, 8vo., *price 3s.*—A mezzotinto of the author, by the ingenious Mr. Earlom, (whose industry and abilities do honor to the rising arts of Great Britain), is placed at the head of it. We should have been glad, indeed, to have some better proofs concerning the authenticity of the original, than a bare assertion that it was painted by Cornelius Jansen, and is to be found in a private collection, which we are not easily inclined to treat with much respect, especially as we hear it is filled with the performances of one of the most contemptible daubers of the age." In a note the reviewer gives Walpole's assertion that Jansen's first works in England are dated about 1618 and refers to the date 1610 on this picture. He then proceeds to assert that "the only true picture of Shakespeare supposed to be now extant" is the Chandos portrait. The review is throughout very abusive of Mr. Jennens' edition of *King Lear*.

The subsequent number of the *Critical Review* (for January, 1771,) contained the following additional notice of Earlom's engraving:

"Concerning this print we will have no controversy; but we still adhere to our former opinion, that the soul of the mezzotinto is not the soul of Shakespeare. It has been the fate of Shakespeare to have many mistakes committed both about his soul and body: Pope exhibited him under the form of James the First."*

To these criticisms Jennens replied at length, defending his edition, and the engraving which accompanied it. Referring to the latter he said:

"Concerning the authenticity of the picture from which the mezzotinto print of Shakespeare was taken, they have dropped the controversy; and we are very glad that they had so much sense and modesty left as to find out what impudence and absurdity they have been guilty of, in calling in question a picture they have never seen, and without any provocation abusing a person whom the generality of the world have thought fit to esteem an artist that excels in the higher branches of painting, and of whose performances Mr. Jennens has many, though his

---

* This refers to the engraving by G. Vertue, dated 1721, which was published in Pope's edition of Shakespeare, London: 1725, 4to. It is undoubtedly a picture of James I., though purporting to represent Shakespeare.

collection cannot be said to be *filled with them* (as the Critical Reviewers say they hear), their number being inconsiderable when compared with the whole collection.

"They say, 'we still adhere to our former opinion, that the soul of the mezzotinto is not the soul of Shakespeare.' Who said it was? The soul of a picture cannot be the soul of a man; but a picture may be *like* a man's soul, when it is made to express those qualities and dispositions which we discover him by his writings to have been possessed of." *

Here Mr. Jennens ended, and he gives no information as to where the picture came from, or even the names of any of the other pictures in his possession which he considered to also be by Jansen.

It is to be presumed that Jennens obtained this portrait sometime after 1761, because in a book then published, entitled *London and its Environs*, a careful catalogue of the pictures at his house in Great Ormond Street is given. In this catalogue the only portrait of Shakespeare mentioned is a drawing in crayon, by Vander

---

* *The Tragedy of King Lear, as lately published, Vindicated from the Abuse of the Critical Reviewers; and the Wonderful Genius and Abilities of those Gentlemen for Criticism, set forth, celebrated, and extolled, by the Editor of King Lear.* London: 1772, 8vo., p. 36.

Gucht, from the Chandos portrait. In 1770, it will be remembered, the mezzotint by Earlom from the picture, in Jennens' possession, was published, so that in all probability he acquired it between 1761 and 1770, because his elegant residence at Gopsal, in Leicestershire, was built, it is believed, shortly before 1770. In 1773 Jennens died, and the Gopsal house passed into the hands of Mr. Penn Asheton Curzon, who was the husband of a niece of Mr. Jennens.

Boaden, prior to 1824, inquired of Earl Howe, the then owner of Gopsal, if the picture was in the collection there, and was informed that the only portrait of Shakespeare in the collection was the crayon drawing by Vander Gucht, from the Chandos portrait, above referred to. After further search Boaden found it in the possession of the Duke of Somerset. From this nobleman it obtained the name it sometimes bears—"the Somerset portrait."

Boaden further informs us that the Duke of Somerset received the portrait as a present from the then Duke of Hamilton, and he continues, he has "unquestionable authority" (which, unfortunately, he does not give,) "for saying that it came up with a considerable part of the collection from Gopsal, and was bought by Woodburn for His Grace the Duke of Hamilton, somewhere about fifteen years back."*

This would make the date of Woodburn's purchase about 1809, as the above statement of Boaden's was published in 1824. In 1811 S. Woodburn published a wretched print engraved by R. Dunkarton, from the Jansen portrait, which is stated to be "from an original picture formerly in the possession of Prince Rupert, now in the collection of His Grace, Archibald, Duke of Hamilton and Brandon &c., &c., at Marylebone Park, London." The face is an entire failure and represents the complexion as dark as a mulatto. The expression is much altered, the ruff badly drawn, the costume blotched all over, and the hair looks like a wig.

This would seem to establish, beyond all doubt, that in 1811, the Jansen portrait was in the possession of the then Duke of Hamilton.

Wivell tells us that he called on Samuel Woodburn, the son of the Mr. Woodburn who Boaden states purchased the picture for the Duke of Hamilton. Woodburn's account, as given by Wivell, is that the portrait formerly belonged to Prince Rupert, who left it to his natural daughter Ruperta. This lady was the child of

---

* *An Inquiry*, etc. London: 1824, 8vo., p. 193.

Margaret Hughes, the mistress of the prince. She married Mr. Emmanuel Scroope Howe. Their descendants sold all the pictures, including the Jansen portrait, to a Mr. Spackman, a picture dealer, from whom the father of Mr. Samuel Woodburn purchased it. He kept it for two years, and then sold it to the Duke of Hamilton, who afterwards presented it to his daughter, the Duchess of Somerset. It will be noticed that Woodburn's account ignores Mr. Jennens' possession of the picture.

Boaden had the picture taken down from the wall for his inspection, and says that it is on panel, and that the oak on which it is painted had then (prior to 1824,) commenced to split in two places. He continues: "It is no made up questionable thing, like so many that are foisted upon us. It is an early picture by Cornelius Jansen, tenderly and beautifully painted. Time seems to have treated it with infinite kindness; for it is quite pure, and exhibits its original surface. The epithet *gentle*, which contemporary fondness attached to the name of Shakespeare, seems to be fully justified by the likeness before us. The expression of the countenance really equals the demand of the fancy; and you feel that everything was possible to a being so happily constituted."*

---

* *An Inquiry*, etc. London, 1824, 8vo., p. 194.

Wivell (prior to 1827) also saw this picture, and says that the panel on which it is painted is split in two places, one of which is in the forehead.

The picture is beautifully painted in a neat and delicate manner, and of all representations of Shakespeare it is the most artistic. The expression is singularly soft and mild and the face very refined. It more nearly resembles the Death Mask than any of the other portraits. The costume is exceedingly rich, the ruff very elaborate, and it has been supposed to be either a theatrical costume or a court dress.

Immediately above the head, on a scroll, in Earlom's mezzotint, are the words "Ut magus." These are evidently part of Horace's Epistle to Augustus, to be found in Epistle I, Book 2, lines 208 to 213:

> "Ac ne forte putes, me, quæ facere ipse recusem,
> Cum recte tractent alii, laudare maligne;
> Ille per extentum funem mihi posse videtur
> Ire poëta; meum qui pectus inaniter angit,
> Irritat, mulcet, falsis terroribus, implet,
> Ut magus; et modo me Thebis, modo ponit Athenis."

Boaden speaks of the words "Ut magus" as being on the Jansen portrait, but Wivell expressly denies this, and states that there is nothing except the age of the person represented, and the date that it was painted.* He thinks that Boaden was misled by the fact of the words "Ut magus" being on Earlom's print. How came it then, that Earlom put them there, or was it a conceit of Jennens?

Friswell repeats Boaden's statement as to these words being on the portrait.

On January 1, 1824, an engraving was published by G. Smeeton, lettered as follows: "Shakespeare, Engraved by R. Cooper, with Permission, from the Original in the Collection of John Wilson Croker, Esqr., M. P." It is in an oval, within a square, and is very well engraved. Boaden saw this print, and was struck with its resemblance to the Jansen portrait. He gives the following account of an interview he had with Mr. Croker:

"Mr. Croker with the utmost readiness indulged my curiosity, and agreeably surprised me by the sight of an absolute *fac-simile* of the Duke's picture. I see no difference whatever in the execution—the character of course is identical. It should, however, be observed, that although the Duke's picture is on panel, Mr. Croker's is on canvas. I must add to this remark, that the picture on canvas has no date or age painted upon it, and that the portrait is an oval within a square; in other words, the

---

* *An Inquiry*, etc. London: 1827, 8vo., p. 242.

angles are rounded off. The mode, Mr. Croker tells me, in which the picture was discovered, was singularly remarkable. It was hidden behind a panel, in one of the houses lately* pulled down near the site of Old Suffolk Street, and he purchased it in a state of comparative filth and decay. It has been very judiciously cleaned and lined, but no second pencil has ever been allowed to touch it. This discovery of pictures behind wainscoting is not unusual, particularly in the country. It was once the practice in plastered walls, to insert frames of the same color, and these formed all the decorations of the pictures. Subsequently when it was determined to wainscot an apartment, the picture was often become so sallow by time and dirt, as to be hardly visible, and was so deemed not worth the trouble of extraction, and therefore covered along with the wall which inclosed it. An instance of this kind comes positively within my own knowledge.

"Had it been possible, I should have pursued the inquiry to the ascertainment of the identical house from which it came, and thus at all events have tried to trace out its ancient possessor. But Mr. Croker could give me no further detail. He received the account without

---

* This statement was published in 1824.

suspicion, for the picture was obviously ancient, and from its condition, had as obviously been hidden. He bought it liberally, and has reason to congratulate himself upon the acquisition."* What has become of Mr. Croker's copy is not known.

Many engravers have tried their skill in copying the Jansen portrait. Earlom was the first. His beautiful mezzotint, published in 1770, as the frontispiece of Jennens' edition of *King Lear*, has already been referred to. Earlom's copy, though very well engraved, is not a faithful representation of the picture. He has made the forehead lower, altered the shape of the head, and changed the mouth. The costume is but faintly indicated in this print. The scroll with "Ut magus" which appears in this mezzotint has already been referred to.

Gardner next engraved a small oval plate for *The Literary Magazine*, which was published June 1, 1793, by J. Good. He reversed the head, changed the expression, and preserved none of the beauty of Earlom's mezzotint, from which he evidently copied. It is a very poor engraving, and omits the "Ut magus," the date, and the age.

Woodburn's print, engraved by R. Dunkarton, and

---

* *An Inquiry*, etc. London: 1824, 8vo., p. 197.

published in 1811, has been noticed above. The date and age are given, but the "Ut magus" is omitted.

R. Page engraved a small plate representing this portrait in a frame, which was published by John Bumpus, in 1822. Underneath is engraved "Shakspeare, from his monument in St. Mary's Church, Stratford." Its likeness to the Jansen portrait is plainly recognizable, and hence the absurdity of the statement that it is from the Stratford bust; and the publisher evidently did not know that the proper name of the church is the Holy Trinity. No date, age, or inscription is given in this engraving.

R. Cooper next copied this picture, *circa* 1824, with indifferent results. The date, age, and inscription are omitted. This plate must not be confounded with another, by the same engraver, published January 1, 1824, by G. Smeeton. The latter is from Mr. Croker's copy of the Jansen, and has been already described.

The finest engraving ever made from the Jansen portrait is undoubtedly Charles Turner's magnificent mezzotint, published in 1824, by Robert Triphook, and forming one of the illustrations of Boaden's *Inquiry*. It is beautifully engraved in Turner's best manner, and seen in an India proof, as published in the quarto edition of Boaden's work, it is superb. Turner did not give the costume at all; the head and ruff stand out in bold relief on the black background, and the figure can only be faintly traced. The age and date are given very indistinctly, and the scroll bearing the words "Ut magus" is on the margin of the print, above the head. A photograph of this mezzotint was published in Friswell's *Life Portraits*, etc., London: 1864, 8vo.

To turn from this beautiful mezzotint to Page's commonplace little engraving, published by Duncombe, in 1826, is a great change. He gives the date and age, but omits the "Ut magus."

T. Wright copied Earlom's print for Wivell's *Inquiry*, 1827, in which his engraving appeared. It is a poor, spiritless performance, though not utterly lacking in merit. Wivell, however, says that "the etching was first done from Earlom's print, and by permission of his Grace the Duke of Somerset, Mr. Wright and myself have inspected the original painting, from which the plate has been finished, and is what I conceive it to be, a faithful representation of it." * The age and date are given, but the scroll and inscription are omitted. Traces of the "Ut magus" can be faintly seen, but they have been erased by engraving over them.

A miserable plate, engraved by H. Robinson, was pub-

---

* *An Inquiry*, etc. London: 1827, 8vo., p. 244.

lished by Fisher, Son & Co., in 1835. It appeared in Wheler's edition of Shakespeare, dated 1834, although the print has 1835 on it. There is a *fac-simile* of the poet's signature under it.

In *Religious and Moral Sentences Culled from the Works of Shakespeare*, London: 1847, 8vo., there appeared quite a good lithographic copy of Earlom's print. It is by J. R. Jobbins, and gives the age, date, scroll, and inscription.

About this time Griffin & Co. published a well-executed line engraving from this picture. No engraver's name is given, but whoever he was he has managed to change the face so much that it is utterly unlike the portrait. No date, age, or inscription is given.

A curious little engraving by Lacour, a Frenchman, published *circa* 1850, is very unlike the picture it is intended to represent. No age, date, or inscription is shown in the engraving.

About this time a print engraved by Hopwood appeared. He has materially changed the expression of the face, and taken liberties with the costume. No date, age, scroll, nor inscription is given.

G. Greatbach was very unsuccessful in copying this portrait. His plate was published by John Tallis & Co. in their edition of Shakespeare, London and New York, royal 8vo., 1851 (?) The age, date, scroll, and inscription are omitted.

Quite a good copy from Earlom's mezzotint was published in Charles and Mary Cowden Clarke's edition of Shakespeare, London: 1865–69 (?) No engraver's name is stated, and though the age and date are given, the scroll and inscription are omitted.

The Felton Portrait.

FROM ENGRAVING BY T. TROTTER.

THE FELTON PORTRAIT.

ON August 9, 1794, William Richardson, a print-seller, of Castle Street, Leicester Square, London, informed George Steevens, the well-known Shakespearian editor and critic, that S. Felton, of Curzon Street, London, had in his possession an old portrait, which appeared to him to be similar to the Droeshout engraving in the folio editions of Shakespeare. Steevens took such deep interest in everything relating to the great poet, whose works he has done so much to illustrate, that he was naturally very anxious to see this portrait. Mr. Richardson was subsequently allowed by Mr. Felton to bring it to Steevens and show it to him. The latter was much struck with the resemblance between the portrait and Droeshout's plate, and believed, with many others, that it was the original picture from which Droeshout made his engraving. Steevens tells us that the latter "could follow the outlines of a face with tolerable accuracy, but usually left them as hard as if hewn out of a rock. Thus, in the present instance, he has servilely transferred the features of Shakespeare from the painting to the copper, omitting every trait of the mild and benevolent character which his portrait so decidedly affords."

It appears that Mr. Felton purchased this portrait, on May 31, 1792, for five guineas, from J. Wilson, who had a museum in King Street, St. James Square. In the catalogue of "The fourth Exhibition and Sale by private Contract at the European Museum, King Street, St. James' Square, 1792" appears the following entry: "No 359. A curious portrait of Shakespeare, painted in 1597." If Mr. Wilson really believed that it was a genuine portrait of Shakespeare, painted by a contemporary of the poet's, in 1597, it was very singular that he should have been willing to part with it for the small sum of five guineas.

After its purchase by Mr. Felton, the latter desired to obtain some further information concerning its history, and applied to Mr. Wilson for details as to where he had obtained it. In reply the latter wrote him as follows:

"To Mr. S. Felton, Drayton, Shropshire:

"Sir,—The Head of Shakespeare was purchased out of an old house, known by the sign of the Boar, in Eastcheap, London, where Shakespeare and his friends used to resort, and, report says, was painted by a player of that time, but whose name I have not been able to learn.

"I am, Sir, with great regard,
"Your most obed't. servant,
"J. WILSON.
"Sept. 11, 1792."

Wilson, in giving this account, seems to have overlooked the great fire which occurred in London in 1666, which entirely destroyed Eastcheap. It is not at all probable that a picture would have been saved from a conflagration which Evelyn, in his *Memoirs*, says "was so universal, and the people so astonish'd, that, from the beginning, I know not by what despondency or fate, they hardly stirr'd to quench it; so that there was nothing heard or seene but crying out and lamentation, running about like distracted creatures, without at all attempting to save even their goods, such a strange consternation there was upon them."

On August 11, 1794, two years after this letter to Mr. Felton, Mr. Wilson told Steevens a very different story. The latter says that Wilson assured him "that this portrait was found between four and five years ago at a broker's shop in the Minories, by a man of fashion, whose name must be concealed; that it afterwards came (attended by the Eastcheap story, etc.) with a part of that gentleman's collection of paintings, to be sold at the European Museum, and was exhibited there for about three months, during which time it was seen by Lord Leicester and Lord Orford, who both allowed it to be a genuine picture of Shakespeare."

What peculiar qualifications these gentlemen possessed which enabled them to judge of the genuineness of this portrait is not stated, but Steevens takes occasion to remark that "it is natural to suppose that the mutilated state of it prevented either of their Lordships from becoming its purchaser." On the contrary, they allowed Mr. Wilson to buy it for a mere song—as he must have done to enable him to sell it to Mr. Felton for five guineas! It would seem that if these gentlemen really believed it to be a genuine portrait·of Shakespeare they would not have let it be so sacrificed; for the mutilated state of which Steevens speaks, consisted in its having had a portion of the panel of wood on which it is painted split off, and the picture cut down until the head and a portion of the ruff alone remained. The entire countenance, however, was perfect and in fair condition.

Felton sold this picture (which still bears his name) to Mr. G. Nichol for forty guineas. A copy was made

The Felton Portrait.

FROM ENGRAVING BY T. TROTTER.

from it by Josiah Boydell for Steevens about this time, which remained in the latter's possession until his death. The original portrait was owned for a long time by Mr. Nichol, and he is said to have refused one hundred guineas for it, which was offered by Lord Ellesmere.

Subsequently it was in the possession of a Mr. Westmacott, a solicitor, of London, who died in 1861 or 1862. On April 30, 1870, it was offered for sale at public auction in London, and was bought in at fifty guineas. It is not known in whose possession the picture now is.

Such is the history of this portrait, and it will be seen that it is not at all trustworthy. Boswell does not hesitate to say that "there are not, indeed, wanting those who suspect that Mr. Steevens was better acquainted with the history of its manufacture, and that there was a deeper meaning in his words, when he tells us, 'he was instrumental in procuring it,' than he would have wished to be generally understood; and that the fabricator of the Hardiknutian tablet had been trying his ingenuity upon a more important scale. My venerable friend, the late Mr. Bindley, of the Stamp-office, was reluctantly persuaded, by his importunity, to attest his opinion in favor of this picture, which he did in deference to the judgment of one so well acquainted with Shakespeare; but happening to glance his eye upon Mr. Steevens' face, he instantly perceived, by the triumph depicted in the peculiar expression of his countenance, that he had been deceived."*

The portrait is painted on wood, as before stated. On the back of the panel there is the inscription in old-style writing: "Gul. Shakspear, 1597. R. B." The last letters were at first supposed to be "R. N.," but Abraham Wivell (prior to 1827,) when oiling the back of the picture to preserve the wood, discovered that they were really "R. B." Wivell at once concluded that they stood for Richard Burbage, the actor, who was Shakespeare's contemporary, and who is known to have also had some skill as a painter. The final "e" in the poet's name has been lost in cutting off a portion of the wood on which the portrait is painted.

The size of this panel is eleven inches high, and a little over eight inches wide. Boaden says that when he "first saw this head at Richardson's, I found that it had been a good deal rubbed under the eyes; but that there were no circular cracks upon the surface, which time is sure to produce. There was a splitting of the crust of the picture down the nose, which seemed the operation of heat, rather than age. I remember the difficult task Mr. Boy-

---

* Advertisement to Boswell's edition of Malone's Shakespeare. London: 1821, 8vo., Vol. I, p. xxvii.

dell described, when he afterwards, by softening the paint, and pressing with the palette-knife, succeeded in fixing these warped and dissevered parts to the oak panel, on which they originally reposed."*

To this Wivell adds: "The condition of this picture is greatly against its appearance to those who are not able to discriminate and make allowance for such a state, as it is covered all over with dark spots, occasioned by being a long time in a damp place without varnish."†

The picture is well drawn and well colored. The expression is singularly calm and benevolent, and it has been much admired. It resembles the Droeshout engraving more than any other portrait, and by many has been believed to be a copy of it. On the other hand, Steevens thought that it was the original of that engraving. The forehead is much higher than in the Droeshout, and the expression somewhat different, but, as before stated, its resemblance is greater to that portrait than to any other.

The copy made by Josiah Boydell, for Steevens, which has been already referred to, was found by Wivell, (prior to 1827,) in the possession of a Mr. Harris, of London. On the back of this copy is the following:

---

* *An Inquiry*, etc. London: 1824, 8vo., p. 104.
† *An Inquiry*, etc. London: 1827, 8vo., p. 45.

"May, 1797.

"Copied by Josiah Boydell, at my request, from the remains of the only genuine Portrait of William Shakspeare. "George Steevens.

"The original had belonged to Mr. Felton, and is now in the Shakspeare Gallery, Pall Mall."

Mr. Harris bought it at the sale of Steevens' effects for "about three guineas" as he informed Wivell. The latter adds that "it is a very good copy as far as regards the drawing, but the coloring is not so well."*

In 1794, William Richardson, the print-seller above alluded to, issued "proposals" for the publication of two engraved plates of this portrait. These proposals are dated November 5, 1794, and must either have been published before that, or else the date on the engravings is incorrect, for when the latter appeared they bore the date November 1, 1794. Both plates are five and three-quarter inches high and four and a half inches wide, exclusive of the margin. Plate No. 1 represents the picture as it actually is, showing how a portion of the hair and ruff have been split off with the board on which it is painted. The panel has also been cut off just under the ruff, leaving only a very small portion of the dress

---

* *An Inquiry*, etc. London: 1827, 8vo., p. 119.

visible. In this engraving the portion of the hair and ruff cut off have been added in outline, and the figure below the shoulders, in the dress shown in the Droeshout engraving, also added.

Plate No. 2 gives the head exactly as in the former, but the portions of the missing hair and ruff are added, and the dress given as in plate No. 1, but not in outline. Both plates are very well engraved by T. Trotter, and give perhaps the best representation of this picture that can be expected.

Steevens, as before stated, took the greatest interest in the Felton portrait, and wrote the preface and supplement to Richardson's *Proposals* for the publication of these plates. When they were finally published he presented his friend Mr. Chauvel with a pair of the prints as a Christmas present, and wrote on the bottom of one of them "Mr. Chauvel," and on the other "Mr. Chauvel. G. S. Decr. 24." These two engravings are in the present writer's collection.

In 1796 Richardson again had this portrait engraved, this time by J. Godfrey. It is not nearly as good as Trotter's plates, being much larger and coarser, and is a poor representation of the original.

When Isaac Reed's edition of Shakespeare was published, in 1803, by J. Johnson, etc., there was prefixed to it an oval-shaped engraving of this portrait by J. Neagle (March 31, 1803), which is fairly well done, but the expression is not as soft as in the original. Neagle changed the stiff ruff somewhat to make it look more like a linen collar, and the costume that he has added is a plain black gown, entirely different from the Droeshout engraving.

The same year (1803) C. Warren engraved a smaller plate, also in an oval like the preceding one, and evidently copied from it. It is not as well done, however. It is dated May 1, 1803, and was issued by the same publishers as the former (J. Johnson, etc.).

John Thurston made a drawing from this portrait, which was engraved by Charles Warren (the engraver of the preceding plate), and published by James Wallis, July 22, 1805. The head is turned the opposite way to the original, and the nose is very unlike the portrait.

I. Thomson engraved a plate, about this time, which is apparently copied from the preceding one, as it has the same defect in the nose, and the head is also reversed. It has no name of any publisher nor any date.

Manley Wood's edition of Shakespeare, London: 1806, 8vo., contained a well engraved plate by C. Warren. The plate is dated May 1, 1806, and was published by George Kearsley. It is a fair copy of Trotter's plate

No. 2 (1794). It is almost square, and above are emblematical ornaments, while below is "W. Shakspeare." The dress is taken from the Droeshout as is also the case in Trotter's plate. It is said to be "from the original picture," but it is such an exact copy of Trotter's engraving that the statement may well be doubted.

A very poor print, engraved by J. Collyer, was published by J. Nichols and Son, etc., Nov. 30, 1810. It appeared in the edition of Shakespeare, from Steevens' text, published in 1811. It is very coarsely done, and the expression has been much changed.

Reed's edition of Shakespeare, London: 1813, 8vo., contained an engraving of this portrait, by W. Holl. It is of the head only, like the original, and is done in dots. It is fair, but the soft expression of the original has not been fully preserved. It is surrounded by a neat frame. The plate is dated Dec. 26, 1812, and is published "by F. C. & J. Rivington, & the other Proprietors."

A very curious engraving by W. T. Fry, published by Longman & Co., 1819, entirely misrepresents the original. The figure which the engraver has added is out of all proportion, and the face has a sleepy expression.

In 1822 Cosmo Armstrong engraved a small plate from this portrait in which the expression is very different from the painting.

In 1827 Wivell made an engraving of this picture for his work on the portraits of Shakespeare (*An Inquiry*, etc., London: 1827, 8vo.), and had nearly completed it when it met with an accident which ruined the plate. He then employed J. Cochran to engrave one in its stead, which was published in the work referred to. It is very well done, except that the ruff is out of place. The very high forehead of the original painting is well represented in this engraving, and the soft, mild expression of the eyes capitally rendered. It is surrounded by a neatly engraved border, and is a print sure to attract attention among a large collection of engravings of Shakespeare by its striking character.

This plate has been copied by H. Wright Smith for R. Grant White's edition of Shakespeare, Vol. I, published by Little, Brown & Co., Boston, in 1865. It also appeared in White's *Memoirs of the Life of William Shakespeare*, issued by the same publishers in 1866. Mr. Smith's plate is a beautiful engraving, and finer work has seldom been done; but he has made the forehead lower than in the Cochran plate and in the painting, given a more animated expression to the eyes, and corrected Cochran's mistake about the ruff. It has the same border as the latter, and is one of the finest engravings of a portrait of Shakespeare that has ever been executed.

The Stratford Portrait.

FROM PHOTOGRAPH OF ORIGINAL BY CUNDALL, DOWNES & CO.

THE STRATFORD PORTRAIT.

IN the latter part of the year 1860, Mr. Simon Collins, a well-known restorer of pictures, residing in London, went to Stratford-upon-Avon, to remove the white paint which had been daubed over the bust of Shakespeare in the chancel of the Church of the Holy Trinity, in that town. After he had completed his work, Mr. William Oakes Hunt, who was then Town Clerk, employed him to clean some old pictures in his possession.

In the upper portion of the latter gentleman's house Mr. Collins found an old portrait, in a dilapidated state, representing a man with a large black beard and moustache. The beard nearly covered the face, and was so arranged as to utterly disfigure the picture. Mr. Hunt stated that the picture had been in the possession of his family for more than a hundred years, and that his grandfather had purchased it at a sale at Clopton House. So little was it regarded that Mr. Hunt had used it for a target, at which to shoot arrows, when he was a boy.

Something about the appearance of the portrait, however, led Mr. Collins to believe that another picture was underneath the outer covering of paint; and he therefore commenced cleaning a portion of the face, when the beard, which almost entirely covered it, disappeared. He then tried the experiment of cleaning a part of the breast of the figure, and found underneath a black and red costume similar to that on the bust of Shakespeare in the chancel of the Holy Trinity Church. During this cleaning the Rev. Mr. Grenville, then Vicar of Stratford, Mr. Hobbs, Mr. Hunt, the owner of the picture, and other residents of the town, were present.

It was afterwards taken to London by Mr. Collins to complete the restoration. When this was completed, the picture was placed on exhibition in Mr. Collins' studio, and the following handbill was given to those who went to see it:

"PORTRAIT OF SHAKESPEARE.

"A portrait of Shakespeare, painted on canvas, three-quarter life-size, which has been in the family of W. O. Hunt, Esq., Town Clerk of Stratford-upon-Avon, for a century, has recently been put into the hands of Mr. Simon Collins, of 6 Somerset Street, Portman Square, London (now on a visit to Stratford), who, after removing the dirt, damp, and repaint by which it was obscured, has brought to light what he pronounces to be a genuine portrait of the Immortal Bard.

"The picture bears a remarkable resemblance to the bust in the chancel of Stratford Church, according to the description given of it before it was painted white at the request of Mr. Malone in 1793, viz.: 'the eyes being of a light hazel, and the hair and beard auburn, the dress consisted of a scarlet doublet, over which was a loose black gown without sleeves.'

"It is important to observe that this is the only picture ever discovered which thus represents the Poet in this dress, and it calls to mind a remark made by Mr. Wheler, in his *History of Stratford-upon-Avon*, of the probability of a picture being in existence from which the monumental bust was taken; which suggestion Mr. Wivell, in his *Inquiry into the History and Antiquities of the Shakespeare Portraits*, quotes, and appears to adopt.

"This picture came into the hands of the present owner (through his father) from his grandfather, William Hunt, Esq., to whom it probably passed, with some other old paintings, in the purchase of his house from the Clopton Family in 1758. The house had then been uninhabited for several years, since the death of its former owner and occupier, Edward Clopton Esq. (nephew of Sir Hugh Clopton), which took place in 1753."

When Mr. Collins had finished cleaning the picture, but before it was taken to London to be "restored," some photographs of it were taken by a Stratford photographer. Using one of these photographs, Mr. John Rabone, of Birmingham, had a large painting executed, of the same size as the original portrait. This copy is of great value, as it represents the original as it was immediately after Mr. Collins cleaned it, and before it had been retouched in the process of restoration. Mr. Rabone states that the latter process has caused much alteration in the original portrait. His copy agrees in all particulars with the photographs taken by the Stratford photographer immediately after the portrait was cleaned. In his copy the lines follow this first photograph exactly, and the expression of the face, as it originally was, is faithfully reproduced. The pose of the figure is now somewhat different, and the face has been altered.

When the picture was returned to Stratford, after undergoing this "restoration," the members of the Birmingham Archæological Association went there to see it. In a lecture lately delivered in Birmingham, by Mr. Rabone, on the portraits of Shakespeare, he referred to this visit and said: "It was in the little theatre which then stood on the site of New Place, and beside it was placed a model of the bust in the church, in colors, just as it had been left from the cleaning. Mr. Collins, who was present, on being questioned about the picture, said he was not there to say what he had done to it, except that he had used every means of his art to make the picture as perfect and as near as was possible to what it was originally, and all he had to say was that the results were before them. It was in a very dilapidated condition, and he had done his best to restore it. A good deal of criticism took place. It was very evident that there was considerable similarity between the painting and the bust. The colors were the same, and the creases and folds in the dress in the one exactly resembled those in the other, from which it was concluded that the painting had been copied from the bust, or the bust from the painting. It was pointed out that the painting contained numerous little life-like points which were altogether wanting in the bust, and therefore it was generally thought more probable that, as the bust had been made by a mere 'tomb-maker,' as Gerard Johnson was, it would be unlikely that those delicate little touches in the painting should be reproduced by him in the stone."*

When the picture was first discovered it excited great interest, and much discussion took place as to whether

---

* *A Lecture on Some Portraits of Shakespeare*, etc. Birmingham: 1884, 8vo., p. 10.

it was the original picture from which the Stratford bust was made, or only a copy from the latter. For there is certainly a very strong resemblance between the two, and the costume of the one is exactly reproduced in the other. The curls of the hair, the arrangement of the beard, and the general coloring of the two also exactly correspond. Such resemblance shows that either the bust was made from the picture, or the picture from the bust, unless indeed both were made from life. That the bust was sculptured during Shakespeare's lifetime no one has suggested—on the contrary, the universal opinion is that it was made after his death, and many have thought from a death mask. The majority of those who have discussed this subject have said that the Stratford portrait was painted long after the bust was made, and that the picture was copied from the bust. This the present writer thinks exceedingly probable—indeed almost certain, although not capable of actual proof. The portrait does not seem to be of sufficient age to warrant any other conclusion.

In 1769 Garrick was the originator of a "jubilee" at Stratford-upon-Avon, during which there occurred processions of persons representing the characters of Shakespeare's plays, dramatic performances in a building erected for that purpose, and other observances. It was a great time for Stratford, and elaborate preparations were made by the townspeople, as well as by those who came from London. It is very probable that the Stratford portrait was painted from the bust in the church at that time, and afterwards preserved, either for its own merits, or as a relic of the jubilee.

But how can the strange condition in which it was found by Mr. Collins be accounted for? Who painted over the face with a full beard, and disguised the red and black costume of the figure? The high respectability of Mr. William Oakes Hunt and his father, in whose possession the portrait was for many years, forbids the idea of any deception from that quarter. It has been suggested that it was thus painted over in Puritanical times to preserve it, as it is well known many other portraits have been treated when players were unpopular. The apparent modernness of the portrait, however, renders this conjecture most improbable.

Mr. Charles Wright was a strong believer in the genuineness of this picture. *The Athenæum* of March 30, 1861, contained an article criticising the portrait very severely, in which the writer stated that it had "no merit of any kind, not even that of age; it is a modern daub, possibly a tavern sign, a 'Shakespeare's Head,' probably made up for some purpose connected with the jubilee."

This criticism offended Mr. Wright, who wrote a letter to the London *Times*, dated April 2, 1861. In this he takes the *Athenæum* writer to task. Subsequently he wrote two other letters to *The Times*, dated April 12, and April 22, 1861, neither of which that journal published. He, therefore, printed them in pamphlet form, and also a longer pamphlet on the Stratford portrait, dated May 31, 1861. In all of these he warmly advocates the claims of this portrait to be considered as an original one.

About this time Mr. J. O. Halliwell-Phillipps wrote: "It is very clear that either the bust was copied from the painting, or the painting from the bust; but having seen the picture, I cannot for a moment longer imagine that the former position can be ultimately established, and I fancy that it is one somewhat unlikely in itself to be correct, even were the painting of the requisite antiquity. I have little, if any, doubt that *this portrait was copied from the bust*, at the very earliest, some time in the first half of the last century, but more probably, as Mr. Dixon has suggested, about the time of the Jubilee. As a memento of the last-named event, it is one of interest and even of pecuniary value; but that interest and value will be absorbed in an estimation of another kind if an attempt be made to give it the precedence of the bust. I can only say that Gertrude's son never so astonished his mother as the sight of that picture astonished me, when it put to flight an expectation to see what so many have desired to behold, yet have never seen."

Among the few favorable criticisms of this portrait was one contained in *The Examiner* of May 18, 1861. That journal remarked concerning the similarity between the bust and the portrait, said: "But nothing in the portrait suggests that it was copied from the bust. The lower part, of course, does not follow the manner of the statuary, and from that fact no conclusion can be drawn. But in the face lies the main evidence. The picture is of such small value as artist's work, that we hardly can credit the painter with the power he must have had of turning stone into life when he added expression in the play of feature to the corners of the mouth, and achieved a successful transformation of the nose. Shakespeare has in the portrait a nose in good harmony with the rest of his face, not insignificant, as on the bust, and differing in outline, especially by a well-marked curve between the root and the tip that in a copyist from the bust would have been an error hardly probable. As a suggestion of the face of Shakespeare the portrait is to be preferred, and there is nothing stony in its look, nothing to discredit at first sight any belief that it may have been a copy from life by one who was a tolerably faithful, although not a first-rate, portrait-painter. The bust, as our readers know, was modelled some time after death, when use was to be made of all possible aids to memory."

The portrait is evidently not the work of an artist of much ability, and yet there are good points in it. The eyes are well done, and have a good expression. The picture represents Shakespeare in the prime of life. The moustache is very small, and curled upwards, as in the bust. The tuft on the chin, also, corresponds to that on the effigy. The costume is very similar.

Mr. Hunt was said to have been offered three thousand pounds for the picture by Mr. Jeremiah Matthews, of Birmingham, but he presented it to the town of Stratford-upon-Avon, where it is preserved in the house on Henley Street, where the poet was born. It is there kept in a fire-proof case, and the frame surrounding it is made from oak taken from the house. Above the frame there is the following inscription on a brass plate:

"This portrait of Shakespeare, after being in the possession of Mr. William Oakes Hunt, Town Clerk of Stratford, and his family, for upwards of a century, was restored to its original condition by Mr. Simon Collins, of London, and being considered a portrait of much interest and value, was given by Mr. Hunt to the town of Strat-

The Stratford Portrait.

From Photograph of Original.

ford-upon-Avon, to be placed and preserved in Shakespeare's house.—23d April, 1862."

There is painted on the case of the frame the following inscription: "This case was made from a portion of the waste wood which formed part of the old structure of Shakespeare's house."

Inside the iron doors of the fire-proof case in which the picture is kept, there are silver plates, bearing the familiar lines from *The Merchant of Venice:*

> "Fast bind, fast find;
> A proverb never stale in thrifty mind."

In March, 1861, Mr. Simon Collins published a large photograph of this picture which represents the portrait as entirely different in expression from its present condition. The negative has been much "touched up" and altered. Indeed it is not generally known how great a change in the expression of a face can be made in a photograph by this process. Dr. C. M. Ingleby was desirous of obtaining a photograph which would represent correctly the Stratford portrait, and went to a great deal of trouble to attain his object, only to meet with utter failure. He took one of Mr. Collins' photographs, referred to above, which was painted upon by Mr. Collins, after the original picture, and then photographed again. The result was painted upon by Mr. Munns, of Birmingham, after the original, and then photographed by H. J. Whitlock. Dr. Ingleby then took the last-named photograph to Stratford-upon-Avon in October, 1872, and compared it with the original picture. He says that he was unable to discover the slightest resemblance between the two faces. The present writer is not surprised at this, for anything more unlike the painting can hardly be imagined. The whole expression of the face has been changed by the repeated "touching up" that it has undergone, and it looks like another picture altogether.

The best photograph of the Stratford portrait, in its present condition, was published in Friswell's *Life Portraits of William Shakespeare;* although the prints in different copies of the book vary very much, they having been printed from a number of negatives, and some of the latter have been more successfully "touched up" than others. They are by Cundall, Downes & Co.

Photographs, purporting to be taken from the Stratford portrait, are sold in Stratford-upon-Avon, as correct delineations of the picture. Some of them show the picture and the frame, and others omit the latter. All of them show the hair frizzed in the most peculiar manner, utterly unlike the curling locks of the painting itself. This, of course, is the result of injudicious alterations of the negatives. The eyebrows are also lengthened, and a new background supplied, the lights and shadows altered, and many minor changes made. In frizzing the hair in these pictures it has been brought further forward, and the expression of the whole face thus altered. They were photographed by F. Bedford, and serve to show how unreliable photographs sometimes are, and yet being the result of a mechanical process, many people think they must be accurate. The likenesses of our friends tell us, however, that this is often not true.

THE ASHBORNE PORTRAIT.

THIS singular portrait has no pedigree. It was purchased by Mr. Clements Kingston, of Ashborne, Derbyshire, England, some time prior to March, 1847. All that is known concerning it is set forth in the following letter written by Mr. Kingston to Mr. Abraham Wivell, author of *An Inquiry*, etc. It has never before been published:

"Grammar School, Ashborne, March 8, 1847.
"Dear Sir:

"I return you many thanks for your kind offer, and also for the candid and open manner in which you express yourself. I am perfectly aware of the innumerable deceptions and frauds of every possible kind which are practiced upon the unwary connoisseur, having given my attention to paintings for the last ten or fifteen years; but I am happy to say nothing of the kind has taken place with regard to the picture in question.

"The way in which I happened to come into possession of it was this: A friend in London sent me word

The Ashborne Portrait.

From Mezzotint by G. F. Storm.

that he had seen a portrait of Shakespeare, that he was positive it was a genuine picture, and that the owner only valued it as being a very fine painting. Being too poor to purchase it for himself, he advised me by all means to have it. I immediately wrote back requesting him to secure me the prize.

"Since being in my possession it has been merely re-lined, and is in most excellent preservation. Of the genuineness of it I have not the slightest doubt whatever, or I should not have asked so valuable an opinion as yours. In fact, and I speak it with the utmost confidence (though I am sure you will consider me too bold), I really believe it to be the best, and certainly the most interesting portrait of the immortal bard in existence.

"The size of the picture is three feet ten inches, by three feet, and represents him, the size of life, down to the knee. His right arm is leaning upon a skull, and in that hand he holds a book, upon the cover of which, amongst the ornamental details, is the crest of the Shakespeare family, and the tragic mask. This is too small to have been put on by any party wishing to pass the portrait off as genuine; for ninety-nine out of a hundred would never notice it; and moreover I will warrant every portion of the picture to have been painted at the same period.

"In the left hand upper corner, in characters of the

period, is Ætatis svæ. 47 A° 1611. The shape of the face and countenance altogether greatly resemble those in the picture belonging to the Duke of Somerset; in fact so very similar do they appear, that, judging from the engraving, I could fancy the two portraits to be the production of the same hand, but the original picture belonging to the Duke I have not seen.

"To sum up, I will warrant my picture to have been purchased in its original state, and that the canvas, etc., is peculiarly of the period in which Shakespeare lived; that it has never been retouched since it was painted, and therefore that whatever detail there may be on it (which I consider gives more weight than anything), was certainly every touch, painted with the portrait itself.

"Should you, after this description, think the matter worthy of your further attention, I will either arrange for the picture being sent to you, or if you will oblige me by saying what your travelling expenses would be, I will send you the sum required.

"In the mean time, I remain, dear sir,

"In haste,

"Yours very truly, and greatly obliged

"CLEMENTS KINGSTON."

"MR. WIVELL."*

---

* This letter is printed from a MS. copy kindly furnished by Samuel Timmins, Esq., J. P.

It will be seen that its history amounts to nothing, and while Mr. Kingston evidently had a strong belief in the genuineness and antiquity of the picture, he had no evidence to support this belief beyond the painting itself.

The portrait is a three-quarter length, and represents Shakespeare standing by a large table, with a cover. He leans his right arm on the table, on one corner of which is a human skull. In the poet's right hand is a book, elaborately bound, with ribbons to tie it together, in the old style. The left hand has a large signet ring on the thumb, and holds an elaborately embroidered gauntlet. The dress is of the Elizabethan style, and consists of a tightly fitting coat, of rich material, but not embroidered, with short waist, and puffed out breeches. A narrow but handsomely worked sword belt encircles the waist, but no sword is shown. A large ruff made of many rows of lace, and smaller ones at the wrists complete the costume.

In the upper left hand corner of the picture, above the right shoulder of the figure, are the words "Ætatis svæ. 47 A° 1611." The forehead is high and somewhat like the Jansen portrait. The eyebrows are delicate and arched, the nose long and not unlike the Jansen, and the mouth also bears a resemblance to that picture. But here the resemblance ends, for while the moustache and beard are the same as in that portrait, the lower part of the face is longer and narrower. In fact the lower part of the head does not seem well drawn, and is unsatisfactory. The expression is sad, and the whole picture, owing to its costume and accessories perhaps, is a striking one. The hands are well drawn except the thumb of the left hand, which is unnaturally long, and on this thumb is a large ring.

On January 1, 1846, a large and beautifully executed mezzotint of this picture, by G. F. Storm, was "published for the proprietor," by the engraver. It states that it is "from an original picture in the possession of C. U. Kingston Esq." It is a somewhat rare print, and is seldom seen. It is beautifully engraved, and represents the picture correctly. The tragic mask which is referred to by Mr. Kingston as being among the ornamental details of the binding of the book, is plainly perceptible in this engraving; but the crest of Shakespeare which he also says is on the binding of the book is not shown.

Shortly after the mezzotint was published, an engraving on wood, copied from it, appeared; and apart from the fact that the engraver has placed the skull directly under the poet's arm instead of on the corner of the table, it is a good copy of Storm's engraving.

Another copy of Storm's mezzotint, this time on steel,

was also published about this time. It is a small plate, but exceeding well engraved, mostly in line. The figure is only shown to the waist, and the table, skull, glove, etc., are omitted. No engraver's or publisher's name is given, and the date of publication is also omitted. Underneath the plate is engraved a fac-simile of Shakespeare's autograph.

THE DUKE OF DEVONSHIRE BUST.

THERE formerly stood in Portugal Street, on the south side of Lincoln's Inn Fields, London, an old red brick building, which was originally called the Duke's Theatre. It was so named after James, Duke of York, the brother of Charles II., and was erected in 1662 for Sir William D'Avenant's company.

D'Avenant, who was born in 1606, was the son of a tavern keeper at Oxford, at whose inn (the "Crown") Shakespeare is said to have been in the habit of stopping when going to and fro between Stratford and London. The story which makes D'Avenant the natural son of the great poet need not be dwelt on here. Certain it is, however, that he always had a great admiration for Shakespeare and his works, and it is related of him that he composed an ode on the poet's death when only ten years old. His first dramatic production is dated 1629, and when Ben Jonson died, in 1637, he was appointed

The Duke of Devonshire Bust.

From Photograph of Original.

The Type of Tregennis' Soul.

By Ho Als. C.

Poet Laureate. Later, during the Civil War, he was accused of being concerned in intrigues, and imprisoned in the Tower of London. He succeeded in escaping to France, however, and returned to England, where he did such good service for the Royalist cause that King Charles made him a knight. D'Avenant was again thrown into prison by his enemies, and, after remaining in the Tower for two years more, he was finally released at the request of Milton. He then established his theatre, which, as before stated, was named the Duke's Theatre. Here he produced many of Shakespeare's plays, but his love for his reputed father's immortal works did not prevent him from making many injudicious changes and alterations in them. One of the best known of these is his version of *Macbeth*, published in 1674. The title-page reads thus: "Macbeth, a Tragædy. With all the Alterations, Amendments, Additions, and New Songs. As it's now Acted at the Dukes Theatre. London, Printed for P. Chetwin, and are to be Sold by most Booksellers, 1674."

In 1737 the Duke's Theatre ceased to be occupied for theatrical performances. It was afterwards altered into a warehouse for Spode and Copeland—names that will ever be dear to the lover of old china. In 1845 the warehouse was pulled down to make additional room for an enlargement of the museum of the College of Surgeons. While the building was being demolished much of the plan and shape of the former theatre was laid bare; and when the workmen were knocking down a portion of one of the walls, on one side of an arched door, that was formerly one of the main entrances to the old theatre, they noticed, among the bricks and mortar that had fallen, broken pieces of a terra-cotta bust. Calling the Curator of the museum of the College of Surgeons adjoining, they pointed out to him these remains. Mr. William Clift, F.R.S., who was then Curator, and his son-in-law, Professor Owen, collected the pieces, and putting them together, they at once saw the bust was well made. Who it was they were not certain, but finally concluded that it was intended for Ben Jonson. Having found a bust on one side of the door, they thought there might be another companion bust on the other side. They therefore directed the workmen to use great care in taking down the portion of the wall that was still standing. Here behind the bricks, a terra-cotta bust, which was at once recognized as that of Shakespeare, was found. It was in a perfect state of preservation, and after it had been carefully cleaned it was in some manner obtained by Mr. Clift. It is very strange that the College of Surgeons did not claim so valuable and interesting a memorial as their own property. Perhaps, however, it was not then thought to be of much importance.

The position in which it was found, bricked up behind a wall that had evidently been erected in converting the old Duke's Theatre into the china warehouse, gives the bust every right to be regarded as a work of the time of Charles I., or a few years later, but there is no mark on it to indicate the date when it was made, and nothing is known of its sculptor.

On the death of Mr. Clift the bust passed to his son-in-law, Professor Owen, afterwards connected with the British Museum. He kept it in his possession for several years, and then sold it, for three hundred guineas, to the Duke of Devonshire. (It will be remembered that the Earl of Ellesmere only paid three hundred and fifty-five guineas for the celebrated Chandos portrait of Shakespeare, when he bought it at the sale of the Duke of Buckingham's effects in 1848.)

The Duke of Devonshire had two casts made from it, one of which he presented to Sir Joseph Paxton, of Crystal Palace fame. In 1864 this cast was at the Crystal Palace, Sydenham, and it is believed to be still there. The original bust was presented to the Garrick Club, King Street, London, in 1855, by the Duke of Devonshire, accompanied by the following letter:

"Brighton, 8th Dec., 1855.

"Sir:

"I have for some time wished to pay a visit to the Garrick Club, and to ask you to show me that most interesting collection which belongs to it; but having again left London for some time, another delay is caused, and I must write to you to say that there is in my possession a very interesting bust of Shakespeare, which I wish to present to the Club as a token of good-will, and also of regret that the state of my health has hitherto obliged me to appear so remiss as a president.

"The bust, which is in terra cotta, was in the possession of Professor Owen, of the College of Surgeons, from whom I purchased it. It was discovered in pulling down the old Duke's Theatre, in Lincoln's Inn Fields, where it was placed under one of the stage-doors; the bust of Ben Jonson (accidentally destroyed by the workmen), occupying a corresponding place over the other door, Shakespeare having been rescued by the timely interposition of Mr. Clift (Professor Owen's father-in-law). The bust became his property, and was given by him to Professor Owen.

"It is my wish to know at what time it will be convenient for the bust to be received; and Sir Joseph Paxton, in whose possession the bust now is, at Sydenham, will forward it at any time if you will inform him or me at what time it should be sent.

"I have the honor to be, sir,

"Your obedient, humble servant,

"DEVONSHIRE.

"J. BARNES, ESQ., *Secretary of the Garrick Club.*"

At the first glance at the bust one would suppose that its features were copied after the Chandos portrait, but a longer inspection shows that it has a much nobler aspect and more closely resembles the Death Mask. There are no ear-rings in the ears, as there are in the Chandos, but the beard on the bust is very much like that in the painting, except that the moustache of the bust is drooping, instead of turned up as in the Chandos. The forehead is high and noble; the hair profuse and curling, like the Chandos. The eyes are fine and well sculptured, the nose sharp and delicately chiselled, but while there is none of the sad expression so painfully well rendered in the Death Mask, and the face is not as broad as the latter, still there is a resemblance to it. The costume is very graceful, and while the elaborate lace collar is evidently of the time of Charles I., the cloak thrown over one shoulder gives the whole figure somewhat of a theatrical appearance.

Its merits as a work of art are quite good, and it is

much superior to the Stratford bust. There is an intellectual expression about the face that makes one wish this was a well authenticated likeness of the great poet.

As to the date of its production nothing certain is known, but it was probably made in the time of Charles I. or his successor. D'Avenant would not have permitted a bust of Shakespeare to ornament his theatre which was utterly unlike the poet, who he claimed as a father, if tradition be true. It will further be remembered that the Chandos portrait was also said to have been in D'Avenant's possession. This bust still remains in the possession of the Garrick Club, and is one of its most interesting relics.

THE HAMPTON COURT PORTRAIT.

IN Hampton Court Palace, situated in the village of Hampton, a few miles from London, is an old painting which formerly hung near the top of a large room with a high ceiling. It was so high from the ground that it was difficult to say what it was. Later it was hung lower, and is now claimed to represent Shakespeare.

The picture is reported to have come from Penhurst, and is stated to have belonged to the D'Lisles; one of whom gave or sold it to William IV., by whom it was placed at Hampton Court. Who painted it is not known, nor indeed can the brief pedigree above given be vouched for. Nothing is positively known about it except that it has been in the palace for many years.

Hampton Court Palace was originally erected by Cardinal Wolsey, and was enlarged by Henry VIII. Edward VI. was born there; Charles I. was confined there for some time, and it was also occupied at various times by Cromwell, Charles II., and James II. William III. rebuilt a large portion of it, and the picture gallery contains works by Raphael, Lely, Holbein, Kneller, West and others. There is nothing improbable, therefore, in a portrait of Shakespeare being in the collection.

The picture represents the figure almost to the knees. The face is more like the Chandos portrait than any other, but the nose is longer. The forehead is very similar to that portrait, but the eyes are blue instead of dark brown as in the Chandos, and the hair is nearly black as compared with the auburn or dark brown of the latter. The mouth, moustache and beard on the cheeks and chin are very similar to those of that portrait, but the dress is entirely different. The Hampton Court picture represents a man in a rich dress, elaborately embroidered, and with gold buttons. It is open at the waist, and at the sleeves. Only the top of the breeches can be seen, but they are red, puffed out, and bombasted in the style of James I. A broad belt is worn high upon the waist, elaborately embroidered, and with a large buckle. Suspended from this are a dagger and sword —the right hand of the figure holding the former, and the left supporting the handle of the sword, which has a large pommel, and a gilt basket-hilt. A large ruff completes the costume; and from the left ear, which is pierced, there hangs a double string. Above the head is the inscription "*Ætat. suæ.* 34." The hands are represented with long and pointed fingers, and there are ruffs at the wrists.

It is evidently a genuine portrait, and not a forgery, but whether it represents Shakespeare or not is a matter which will probably never be known.

Some years ago the Arundel Society published a photograph of this portrait which gives a very good representation of it; but the cracks in the varnish show more distinctly in the photograph than in the picture.

THE HILLIARD MINIATURE.

THIS curious little miniature has a history which is apparently authentic, and certainly far better than most of the pictures that claim to represent Shakespeare.

Sir James Bland Burges, who acquired this miniature on the death of his mother, wrote James Boswell, (who edited Malone's edition of Shakespeare, published in 1821,) the following account of its history:

"Lower Brook Street,
"26th June, 1818.

"Dear Boswell:

"I send you the history of my portrait of Shakespeare, which I apprehend will leave no reason to doubt of its authenticity.

"Mr. Somerville, of Edstone, near Stratford-upon-Avon, ancestor of Somerville, author of the *Chase*, &c., lived in habits of intimacy with Shakespeare, particularly

The Hilliard Miniature.

From Engraving by T. W. Harland.

after his retirement from the stage, and had this portrait painted, which, as you will perceive, was richly set, and was carefully preserved by his descendants, till it came to the hands of his great-grandson, the poet, who dying in 1742, without issue, left his estates to my grandfather, Lord Somerville, and gave this miniature to my mother. She valued it very highly, as well for the sake of the donor, as for that of the great genius of which it was the representative; and I well remember that, when I was a boy, its production was not unfrequently a very acceptable reward of my good behavior. After my mother's death, I sought in vain for this and some other family relics, and at length had abandoned all hope of ever finding them, when chance most unexpectedly restored them to me about ten days ago, in consequence of the opening of a bureau which had belonged to my mother, in a private drawer of which, this and the other missing things were found.

"Believe me to be,
"Dear Boswell,
"Yours most truly,
"J. B. BURGES."

Sir James loaned the miniature to Boswell, who says he "submitted it to the inspection of many of the most distinguished members of the Royal Academy, and to several antiquarian friends."

They thought well of it and he concluded to have an engraving made from it for the edition of Malone's Shakespeare that he was about to publish. By the advice of Sir Thomas Lawrence he employed Mr. Agar to engrave a plate for him. This was done, and the print appeared in the second volume of that work, in 1821.

Boaden says that Boswell showed him the miniature, and that it at once struck him "to have been unquestionably painted by Hilliard." Unfortunately, however, he does not tell us the reasons which led him to believe this, and there is nothing known concerning the miniature that supports such a belief, and it will be observed that Sir James does not say a word as to who the painter was. No doubts, however, seem to have troubled Boaden, and he speaks of Hilliard as if he was unquestionably the painter of the miniature, which will go down to posterity as the "Hilliard miniature," though it would have been far better to call it after Burges.

Nicholas Hilliard was born in 1547, and was well known as an artist in England. He continued to paint until a short time before his death, which took place in 1619.

Speaking of Sir James' account of the history of the miniature, Boaden remarks:

"It would be merely rude to ask for more particulars

as to this transmission of the picture, than Sir James has been pleased to give; but I hope I may without offence express some astonishment, that Somerville the poet, a man born almost on the banks of the Avon, glorying in his countryman, and writing occasionally verses to poets on the subjects of poetry, should have in his possession an authentic portrait of Shakespeare, and never allow it to be engraved; and see Mr. Pope publishing to the world a head of King James, and calling it Shakespeare, and never show to him the treasure on which he might so securely have relied."*

Boaden further states that as Somerville's death did not take place until 1742, he must have heard of these matters, and yet he never communicated the fact of his having such a picture in his possession.

The miniature represents the poet with a somewhat receding forehead, which is much lower than in the other portraits; and the hair, which is also lighter, grows forward in the centre of the forehead, and recedes high up at the sides. The moustache is long and brushed out straight, not drooping. The goatee is long, straight and pointed, and the rest of the face is smooth. The nose is straight, the eyes expressive and handsome, the eye-

---

* *An Inquiry*, etc. London: 1824, 8vo., p. 131.

brows arched. The face is full, and the whole effect quite pleasing. There is a large and deep ruff, with lace around the edge, the costume elaborate. The miniature only shows the figure a little below the shoulders.

The first engraving made from this miniature was a small one, by Agar, published June 25, 1821, "by F. C. and J. Rivington & Partners." It appeared in Boswell's edition of Malone's Shakespeare, London: 1821, 8vo., and has been before referred to. It is a good copy of the miniature, and is a neatly executed engraving.

In 1827 B. Holl made an exact copy of the above engraving, for Wivell's *Inquiry*, etc., London: 1827, 8vo., in which it appeared. The engraving is fully as well done as Agar's, and the only perceptible difference is in the costume, which is a little blacker in Holl's print.

In the second edition of Wivell's *Inquiry*, etc., London: 1840, 8vo., a very fine engraving of this miniature was published. It was engraved by T. W. Harland and is twice as large as the plates by Agar and Holl. Comparing it with them one sees how much finer it is. It has a *fac-simile* of the poet's signature under it.

THE WARWICK PORTRAIT.

AMONG the pictures in Warwick Castle, is one which has been there for many years, and which has always been believed to be a portrait of Shakespeare. Its history, however, is unknown, and who painted it, where it came from, and other details which would enable one to decide upon its claims to be a genuine picture of the poet, are unfortunately all matters of conjecture.

He is represented as seated by a table with a white cover. The chair is red with a high back, and Shakespeare appears to be about to write, and looks up as if in meditation. The background is dark, and the costume black, with ruff and sleeve ruffles of white lace. The face is more youthful than in the other portraits, the complexion reddish, the features delicate, and the beard pointed, with moustache. The expression of the face is refined and spirited, according to Dr. Waagen,* who be-

---
* *Treasures of Art in Great Britain.* London: 1854, Vol. III, p. 216.

stows much praise upon the execution of the picture, and says that it is evidently the work of a careful painter, but he does not even venture to guess who the artist was. He believes it to be an original portrait, and it is greatly to be regretted that some details of its history have not been preserved.

The Jennings Miniature.

FROM ENGRAVING BY W. HOLL.

THE JENNINGS MINIATURE.

THIS miniature, painted in oil, was contained in an enamelled gold locket, which was formerly set with pearls. It was the property of H. Constantine Jennings, of Battersea, who had borrowed six or seven hundred pounds on its security, and that of an old missal, from a Mr. Webb. Either the jewels which the locket formerly contained were valuable, or the missal was of great rarity and value, or else Mr. Webb fared badly, for when the miniature and locket were put up for sale at Christie's, in London, in February, 1827, it was bought by Charles Auriol, Esq., for nine and a half guineas. It had also been owned by a Mr. Wise. Jennings claimed to have traced the possession of the miniature back to the Southampton family, but no proof of this exists.

The miniature is neatly painted, and the features well drawn. The forehead is high, the beard full, as in the Chandos portrait; the collar, which is of lace, very large;

the costume white and much ornamented. Only the head and shoulders are shown. Wilson was of opinion that "there appears upon the face of this picture a stamp of undoubted originality,"* and Wivell says "that the picture is intended for the poet, and is of antiquity, I have no doubt."†

On the side of the picture, on the background, is the age, ÆT 33. It is sometimes called the Auriol miniature.

A beautiful engraving of the miniature was made in 1827, by W. Holl, for Wivell's *Inquiry*. The picture was loaned by Mr. Auriol for this purpose, and the engraving is very well executed.

---

* *Shakespeariana.* London: 1827, 16mo., p. xxxvi.
† *An Inquiry*, etc. London: 1827, 8vo., p. 210.

The Burn Portrait.

From Photograph of Original.

The Emin Portrait.

From a miniature in Geneva.

THE BURN PORTRAIT.

GEORGE Adam Burn Esq., of London, is the owner of this curious picture. He states that it has been in his possession for about forty years, and in his family previously. It has been twice publicly exhibited, first in the Gallery of Old Masters at Burlington House, and again at the "Shakespeare Show" held in the Albert Hall, South Kensington, in 1884.

The picture is in oil, on canvas, and is about eighteen inches high by fifteen inches wide. The face is well drawn and has an animated expression. It bears considerable resemblance to the Stratford bust, except that the hair is much more profuse than in the latter. The moustache and goatee are very similar also to the Stratford bust. The dress is indistinct, except the collar, which is of lace, and is very rich. It is open at the front, displaying the neck. What its history is, or who painted it is unknown. It is considered by its owner to be a genuine portrait of the poet.

An outline sketch of it appeared in the *Shakespearian Show Book*, London: 1884, and it has been well photographed.

THE LUMLEY PORTRAIT.

THIS picture originally formed part of the collection of paintings at Lumley Castle, Durham, England. In 1785 the pictures at the Castle were sold at auction. Who purchased the portrait in question is not known, but subsequently it was repurchased, together with a number of other paintings, by the Earl of Scarborough, who was a relative of Lord Lumley, the former owner of Lumley Castle. It remained in the possession of the Earl of Scarborough's family until 1807, when it was again sold, together with other pictures.

The sale of 1807 seems to have been carelessly managed, for many of the portraits of distinguished Englishmen, of which the collection contained a number, were sold without their names being attached. This alleged portrait of Shakespeare shared that fate, and its value was not known to many of those present at the sale. One gentleman there was, however, who recognized the picture, and purchased it. This was Mr. Ralph Waters, of Newcastle. He was an artist, and saw sufficient merit in it to make him desire to own it. It remained in Mr. Waters' possession until his death, when he left it, by will, to his brother. The latter gentleman sold it to Mr. George Rippon, of North Shields. While it was in Mr. Rippon's possession it was taken to New York, and placed in the Exhibition of the Industry of All Nations, held there in 1863. Many persons who saw it in that exhibition supposed that it was the celebrated Chandos portrait, to which it bears considerable resemblance.

In 1864 it was again exhibited, this time at the Tercentenary celebration of Shakespeare's birth, held at Stratford-upon-Avon in April of that year. While there it attracted much attention. In the official catalogue of that exhibition "Mrs. Rippon" is mentioned as the owner. Another account, however, states that George Rippon bequeathed it to Mr. John Fenwick, of Preston House, Tynemouth.

It was advertised to be sold at auction in London, by Christie and Mason, early in December, 1874, but at the sale only £30 was bid, and it was withdrawn. Subsequently it was privately purchased for the Baroness Burdett-Coutts.

John, Lord Lumley, who began the collection of pictures at Lumley Castle, was born in 1534, and died in 1609. Surtees, in his *History of Durham*, Vol. II, p. 155, says that "the portraits described by Pennant, in 1776, at Lumley Castle, are chiefly portraits of illustrious Englishmen, the contemporaries of John, Lord Lumley, who may be fairly deemed the author of the collection."

Hutchinson (*History of Durham*, p. 403,) remarks that "Dr. Stukeley, in his *Iter Boreale* in 1725, says, 'at Lumley Castle is a curious old picture of *Chaucer*, said to be an original'—we could not find any such portrait." From this passage it has been attempted to be argued that Stukeley's allusion to a portrait of Chaucer was a slip of the pen for Shakespeare, and it is certain that when Hutchinson looked for the Chaucer picture none could be found.

The picture is an oil painting, and as before stated, closely resembles the Chandos portrait. The forehead, nose, eyes, and the general arrangement of the hair and beard are all very similar to that portrait, but the chin seems longer in the Lumley, and the beard is not quite as pointed. The linen collar is of the same shape as the Chandos, and its strings hang down in the same manner as those in that portrait. One cannot help feeling that there is some connection between these two pictures, and indeed, the idea that the Lumley picture was the original of the Chandos has been suggested.

The painting bears every evidence of age, and there is a perfect network of cracks visible on the forehead and cheeks. It does not rank as high as the Chandos portrait as a work of art, the eyes especially not being as well painted.

In 1862 Vincent Brooks made a remarkable chromo-lithograph from the Lumley portrait, published in that year by Henry Graves & Co.; having their place of business, oddly enough, at No. 1 Chandos Street, Covent Garden, London. In this chromo-lithograph the cracks in the original picture are reproduced with marvellous fidelity, and it has every appearance of an old painting itself when looked at from a little distance. A close view, of course, shows that the surface is too smooth for an old picture full of cracks as this one is. The deception is so complete, however, that it is related that one of these copies was once sold for forty guineas to a purchaser who thought he was buying the original Lumley portrait. This is hard to believe, especially as Vincent Brooks' name is in the lower right hand corner.

THE BOSTON ART MUSEUM PORTRAIT.

THIS very striking picture has a curious history, which unfortunately cannot be verified.

On the back of the portrait there is the following inscription:

"William Shakespeare.
"Painted by Federigo Zuccaro.
"1595.

"Was Found in 3 Pieces in pulling down an Old House on the Surrey side of the Thames—where stood once the Globe Tavern and Theatre."

It seems that Benjamin Joy, of Boston, while on a visit to Europe, heard of a sale which was to take place at an old house on the Thames, London, where the Globe Theatre had formerly stood. He attended the auction, and purchased this portrait, which had hung over the mantel-piece of the dining room. It was then so black that it was impossible to say who it represented, and it

The Boston Art Museum Portrait.

From Photograph of Original by Sonrel.

was knocked down to Mr. Joy for a small sum. He was attracted by it because it seemed to be as old as the house.

After keeping it for some time, he sent it, (with the frame in which he had bought it,) to his sister Miss Abby Joy, of Boston. The latter employed a Mr. Howarth, an Englishman residing in that city, to clean it. He informed Miss Joy that it was undoubtedly a portrait of Shakespeare, and that it seemed to him to have been painted by Zucchero, and referred to the lace on the collar as being in his style of work. The frame he said was the production of an Italian, as it had the characteristics of frames made in that country.

When Miss Abby Joy died she left this portrait by will to Mrs. Harrison Gray Otis. While in her possession it was beautifully photographed by Sonrel in two ways, one showing the curious openwork frame, and the other merely the picture.

On the death of Mrs. Otis the picture was presented to the Museum of Fine Arts, Boston, where it now is.

The above details were obligingly communicated to the present writer by Gen. Charles G. Loring, of the Museum of Fine Arts, Boston. Gen. Loring says, "I think it well established that it came from the alleged site. It is evidently a portrait of Shakespeare—to ascribe it to Zucchero is guesswork, and further it has been touched up, how much one cannot say, but Howarth was an unconscionable restorer."

The portrait is painted on panel and represents the head and shoulders only. It is evidently the work of an artist of some ability, for the drawing is excellent. The face is long, and the nose straight and well formed. The eyes are expressive and especially well done; on the chin is a long and pointed goatee; and the moustache thin and brushed out straight. The hair is dark and curling, but owing to the color of the background it is not easy to see the manner in which it is represented. The collar is very large and fluted, edged with lace, the pattern of which is plainly shown. There is an appearance about the collar which would seem to indicate that it had been painted over the goatee, or else the beard over the collar—probably the former. There is certainly something wrong about this part of the picture.

This picture cannot be a portrait of Shakespeare from life by Zucchero, because that artist left England in 1580, when the poet was only sixteen years old, and represents a man of at least thirty-five. But attributing it to that artist is mere guesswork, as Gen. Loring very truly observes.

Nothing could be better than Sonrel's photographs of this picture, which give a perfect representation of it.

THE CHALLIS PORTRAIT.

THOMAS Challis, Esq., a banker, residing in West Smithfield, London, purchased this portrait from one of his old clerks. The latter had bought it at an auction sale of the effects of Dr. Black. These meagre details are all that are known concerning it.

It is a three-quarter length portrait, painted in oil, on a panel which is cracked in two places. These cracks have been carefully repaired, and the background and costume of the figure restored. The cracks did not pass through the face, which is in a good state of preservation.

Friswell saw this portrait prior to 1864, and thus describes it: "The head, which is a fine one, looks too narrow for that of Shakespeare. The forehead is high, but not very broad; the complexion fair, with a brown tint; the eyes a dark gray, so shaded that they appear, unless closely looked into, to be hazel; the nose long, thin, and aquiline, approaching to Roman; the upper lip very short, covered with a brown-red moustache; the hair, which curls naturally, is a true red auburn. The look of the portrait is neither so open nor so generous as that of the bust, the Droeshout, or the Chandos portraits. * * * * The mouth and moustache are the features which most resemble the received portraits, with the exception, before stated, that the upper lip is very short.

"The dress is remarkable: a large, wide-spreading, curiously open-worked, Spanish collar, which extends from shoulder to shoulder, and exhibits the neck nearly to the collar-bone, gives a foreign appearance to the picture; nor does the face detract from this appearance. The dress is excellently painted, and is of a slate color, worked, shaded and bound with black. In one corner of the picture we find the date and age, *Æt.* 46, 1610; the age, of course, corresponds with that of Shakespeare at that period. The neck, as we have noticed, much exposed, is ill drawn; with this exception, in both drawing and execution the picture is admirable."*

He further adds that it is evidently a painting of the time of James I., and that it bears a considerable resemblance to the Death Mask.

---

* *Life Portraits*, etc. London: 1864, 8vo., p. 80.

The Zoust Portrait.

From Engraving by W. Holl.

THE ZOUST PORTRAIT.

IN 1725, or thereabouts, a mezzotint by I. Simon was published, which claimed to represent Shakespeare. Underneath the print, it stated that it was from a painting by Zoust, "in the collection of T. Wright, Painter, in Covent Garden." Malone, in his edition of Shakespeare published in 1790, pointed out that if it was the work of Zoust (or Soest) it must have been a copy from some other artist, as the earliest known picture painted in England by Zoust was dated 1657. Another important fact is that Zoust gives his age on the frame of one of his pictures as thirty years in 1667, so that he must have been born in 1637, which was twenty-one years after Shakespeare's death.

Malone also stated that he believed that the picture from which Simon's mezzotint was made was in the possession of Mr. Douglas, of Teddington, near Twickenham. Wivell saw William Douglas, who told him that the picture had been in his family for sixty years, but could not trace it any further—that Garrick and Sir Joshua Reynolds had seen and admired it while in the possession of Mr. Douglas' father, and Sir Joshua was very anxious to become its owner.

Neither Mr. Douglas nor Wivell thought that the former's picture was the one from which Simon made his mezzotint, for Malone stated that the picture was twenty-four inches by twenty, while Douglas' picture was described in a sale catalogue of Sotheby's (by whom it was advertised for sale) as twenty inches by sixteen.*

Douglas' picture was in the possession of Triphook, the London bookseller, for some time, and is described by Boaden as "pleasing and well painted," but not as fine as the original of Simon's print must have been. This original, Boaden believed to be in some one of the houses of the nobility.†

Simon's mezzotint represents a face very different from any of the accepted portraits of Shakespeare. The face has a delicate expression, and is shown in a three-quarter view. The hair is profuse and curling, and of a brown color, covering the top of the head; the beard, which is

---

* *An Inquiry*, etc. London: 1827, 8vo., p. 161.
† *An Inquiry*, etc. London: 1824, 8vo., p. 139.

full, is slight, and the moustache very slight. The collar is somewhat like that of the Chandos portrait, but without strings. The costume is rich, but plainly made.

Wivell states that "Mr. Booth, Bookseller," had a small copy of this portrait by Cosway,* which was purchased at the sale of that artist's effects for about twenty pounds. This same copy is now owned by Mr. Lionel Booth, to whom all lovers of the poet are indebted for his marvellously accurate reprint of the First Folio.

Douglas sold his picture to Sir John Lister Raye, Bart., of "The Grange," near Wakefield, Yorkshire, for four hundred pounds, prior to 1827. This was the largest price ever paid for a portrait of Shakespeare, as the Chandos portrait only sold for three hundred and fifty-five guineas in 1848.

An excellent copy of Simon's mezzotint was engraved by W. Holl, for Wivell's *Inquiry*, 1827.

---

* *An Inquiry*, etc. London: 1827, 8vo., p. 162.

THE ZUCCHERO PORTRAIT.

THIS portrait was formerly in the possession of R. Cosway, R.A., at whose house Boaden saw it. Cosway claimed that it was an original portrait of Shakespeare. It is on panel, and on the back of the picture were the words "Guglielm. Shakespeare."

The picture could not have been painted by Zucchero, for it represents a man of at least thirty years of age, and Shakespeare having been born in 1564, his portrait, representing him of that age, could not be the work of an artist who left England about 1580. The latter came to England, from Flanders, in 1574, and while in Great Britain, painted two portraits of Queen Elizabeth, and one of Queen Mary of Scotland. He remained in England for five or six years, and was compelled to leave the country on account of having painted some of the Pope's officers with asses' ears, over the gate of St. Luke's Church.

The Zucchero Portrait.

From Engraving by W. Holl.

Ein Zierretto Porträt.

Von Leo Berg.

Nothing further is known concerning the history of this portrait. Cosway did not give Boaden any information, beyond his belief that it was an original picture by Zucchero.

The picture is of life size, in an oval, and delicately painted. It represents Shakespeare leaning on his right elbow. His hand supports his head, and the eyes look directly at the observer. They are very singular, being oblique and somewhat like a cat's. The hair is very thick and black, the beard full and dark, while an enormous collar, open very low at the neck, falls over the shoulders. The costume is very plain. On the table on which the poet leans his arm are some papers. Boaden thought it resembled Torquato Tasso more than Shakespeare, judging from the latter's accepted portraits. It certainly is very unlike any portrait of Shakespeare, and the eyes alone are enough to condemn it as a picture of the great poet.

A mezzotint was made from this portrait by Henry Green, which was coarsely done, and very unlike the original picture.

W. Holl engraved a well executed plate from the picture itself, which was published in Wivell's *Inquiry*, in 1827.

THE BOARDMAN MINIATURE.

THIS miniature, which is on copper, is seven and a quarter inches high, and five and a half inches wide. It is enclosed in an old carved oak frame, formerly gilt, but now painted black, and is in the possession of G. W. W. Firth, Esq., a surgeon, residing in Norwich, England. On the top of the frame there is a scroll, with the arms of Shakespeare, his crest, and motto: "Non sanz droict." Underneath the arms appears the following inscription in gilt capital letters:

> OF RIGHTE WE HAYLE THEE MAYSTER OF THE GLOBE;
> THEE WHOM BEN'S VENOM'D SHAFTE OR SNAREFUL PRAISE
> HAVE NEERE HAD POWER TO BEREAVE OR ROBBE
> O' THE POET'S HIGHEST MEEDE, THE LIVING BAYES.

The last words are in larger capitals than the rest, and under them is a sprig of laurel or bay.

The picture represents the figure as far as the knees. Shakespeare is standing, with a pen in his hand, in the favorite style of representing literary composition, which we all know is never seen in real life. The costume resembles that of the Chandos portrait, with linen collar and strings. The eyes are large, the forehead high, the hair a dark brownish black. The moustache is like that of the Stratford bust, and the upper lip also, like that effigy, is long. In fact, the whole appearance of the face very much resembles that of the Stratford bust, but the expression is weaker, and the complexion darker. The background has gold rubbed over it, and a curtain which is represented in the picture also has gold on it. Traces of the gold dust are also to be seen on the eyes and hair. In one corner of the picture is a small sketch of the Globe Theatre, with flag.

It was long the property of Mr. R. R. Boardman, an antiquarian of Norwich. He purchased it of an auctioneer named Izard, and paid in the neighborhood of three hundred pounds for it. An offer of five hundred pounds made by a clergyman named Fisk, was refused by Boardman, who retained possession of it until his death, when it passed to Firth, who was Boardman's trustee. Where Boardman obtained it or any other details of its history are not known.

In 1864, on the celebration of the anniversary of the three hundredth birthday of Shakespeare, at Stratford-upon-Avon, this miniature was exhibited among a large collection of portraits of the poet. It was called the "Norwich portrait" in the official catalogue of the exhibition.

THE STACE PORTRAIT.

MACHELL Stace, from whom this portrait receives its name, was a bookseller and dealer in pictures, who formerly resided in Middle Scotland Yard, London. Prior to 1811 Stace bought the picture from a Mr. Linnell, of Streatham Street, Bloomsbury, who had purchased it of a Mr. Tuffing, Great Queen Street, Lincoln's Inn Fields. It had been sold at auction, with other pictures which belonged to John Graham, Esq. He had purchased it of a Mr. Sathard, who kept a tavern called the "Old Green Dragon Public House." Sathard bought it at a sale at another tavern rejoicing in the classic name of the "Three Pigeons," where it was said to have been for many years. Such is the pedigree of this portrait as given by Stace. Whether it is founded on fact or drawn from his imagination there are now no means of ascertaining.

The first impression on seeing this picture is that the

The Stacc Portrait.

From Engraving by W. Holl.

eyes are too large. The hair is thick and long, the nose fine, and the mouth good. A small moustache and a goatee are all the beard that the figure has. The costume is plain, with a small collar. Stace stated that it represented the poet at the age of thirty-three, but he forgot to tell us how he fixed the exact age.

In 1811 Stace had a large and striking print engraved by Robert Cooper. In addition to this he issued an engraving showing the house where the picture was found, and he either seems to have believed in the authenticity of his portrait, or else he was an adept in the art of deceiving.

In 1827 W. Holl copied Cooper's print for Wivell's *Inquiry*, in which it was published. It is a very good copy.

THE O'CONNELL PORTRAIT.

THIS portrait, which has no history, is in the possession of J. O'Connell, Esq., of Laurel Street, London, who claims that it is the work of Mark Garrard. It is in very dilapidated condition, owing to bad usage and the thinness of the colors and want of body. It is on canvas, is of life size, and represents the figure to the waist. The forehead is high, the eyes of a bluish brown, and the hair and the beard flaxen. Its general appearance is like the Jansen portrait, and the collar is similar. The costume has been touched with gold. Mr. O'Connell is of the opinion that the whole background (which is now reddish brown) was originally gold. The hair has been covered with auburn, but the flaxen color shows in places, and the beard is of the original flaxen tint.

In 1884 it was exhibited at the "Shakespeare Show," in the Albert Hall, London, where it attracted much attention.

Friswell was of opinion that it was probably the work of Garrard, but considered it very doubtful if it was ever intended to represent Shakespeare.

The Gilliland Portrait.

From Engraving by W. Holl.

THE GILLILAND PORTRAIT.

THIS curious portrait was formerly in the possession of Mr. Thomas Gilliland, of London.

It is on canvas, but the latter has been mounted on board. On the back is the following history of the picture:

"This portrait of Shakespeare I cut from a picture about three feet square, containing several other portraits in the same style of work. The picture was recently bought at the Custom House, by a picture dealer, of whom I purchased it, under a strong impression that it was painted about the time of Shakespeare, either by an artist who had seen him, or who copied a genuine portrait of the poet now lost, as this likeness differs from all the portraits hitherto published or known.

"Thomas Gilliland.

"London, April 3, 1827."

The picture is entirely different from all others which have been put forward as portraits of Shakespeare. The face is three-quarter view, the cheek bones are high and prominent, and the cheeks thin. The moustache is full, and the beard a thick bunch on the chin. The hair is quite long and waving. The costume represents a loose gown, with a large plain collar worn over it.

A good engraving of this portrait, by W. Holl, was published in 1827, in Wivell's *Inquiry*. It represents it with fidelity, and shows clearly that the portrait never was intended for a picture of Shakespeare. In nearly all of the others, whether genuine or forged, there can be traced some faint resemblance to the authentic portraits, but in this there is none.

THE HARDIE PORTRAIT.

A VERY singular portrait, purporting to represent Shakespeare, was formerly in the possession of Dr. Hardie, of Manchester, England. At one time it was regarded by some persons as a genuine picture, but Wivell subsequently discovered that it was a forgery by Zincke. He had altered it from the portrait of a French dancing master, which he purchased for a few shillings.

The Literary Journal for October 31, 1818, describes it as being two feet eleven inches by two feet three inches in size, and says that the head is painted in a lozenge shaped shield, "which is suspended in the talons of an eagle, with the following lines, in free old English characters, upon the lozenge, immediately under the head:—

"Ye nutte browne haire, ye fronte serine
Thatte placide mauthe, those smylinge eyne,
Doe soon bewraye my Shakespeare's meine.

"And below that, on an arabesque scroll, are the following:—

> "His thunders lay'de aside, beholde
> Jove's fav'rite birde, now uncontroulled,
> Selecte ye gemme of human race
> And raise himme to th' Empyreane space;
> Fitte statione for his loftie soule
> Whose piercinge eye survey'd ye whole
> Of Nature's vaste domayne,
> Then on Imagination's aierie winge
> Toe worldes unseene yth ardent soule cou'd springe,
> Deepe fraughte t'enriche ye nethere worlde again."
>
> "B. J."

The Literary Journal ascribed these verses to Ben Jonson, but he never wrote such trash. Perhaps Zincke wrote them himself. The portrait was further described as having been well drawn and colored, and bearing a strong resemblance to the Stratford bust.

THE LIDDELL PORTRAIT.

THE Liddell portrait is painted on an oak panel, and is three-quarter size. It was purchased by Thomas Liddell, Esq., of Portland Place, London, from a Mr. Lewis, of Charles Street, Soho, for thirty-nine pounds. It strongly resembles the Stratford bust, but Wivell noticed, when he went to see it (prior to 1827) that the hair, beard, mouth, and ruff seemed to have been altered from their original appearance. Thinking that these alterations might be the work of Edward Holder, who had made many spurious portraits of Shakespeare, he suggested this to Mr. Liddell, and proposed to bring Holder with him again to see the picture. Holder came to Wivell's house, and before the latter had even mentioned Mr. Liddell's name to him, Holder asked whether the picture they were going to see was in that gentleman's possession. While on their way to Mr. Liddell's house Wivell cautioned Holder not to deceive the owner of the picture, but to tell the truth about it. Holder stated that he "had repaired no more than a small place in the cheek, and glazed the hair."

As soon as they entered the room where the picture was, Holder pointed it out, and remarked that he "believed the portrait to be the most perfect and genuine of Shakespeare, and considered its value at two or three hundred pounds." The owner of the picture, however, thought it worth double that sum.

Wivell questioned Holder further, asking him if he had not altered the mouth, the beard, and the ruff. He acknowledged that he had painted on the hair and the ruff, but not the beard. Wivell replied that he must have done so, as it was different from the moustache, which he believed to be genuine.

Finally Holder acknowledged having purchased the picture from a Mr. Bryant, of Great Ormond Street. Going to Bryant, Wivell was informed by him that he had never sold the picture as a portrait of Shakespeare. Later Holder told Wivell that he had bought it at another shop, at the corner of Charles and Oxford Streets. Wivell went there with Holder, and while they were there Bryant happened to come in. He blamed Holder for having wrongfully stated the facts, and Wivell induced Bryant to accompany him to Mr. Liddell's. They went to that gentleman's house, and Bryant said that he was positive that the picture had been altered in the nose, the forehead made higher, the hair repainted, and an ear-ring added. A date which was originally in one corner, and which Bryant stated was after Shakespeare's death, had been painted out since he had had the picture.

On the following day Mr. Liddell called on Wivell and told him that a distinguished artist had assured him that the portrait was a genuine one. An appointment was then made for this artist, Holder, and Wivell to meet at Mr. Liddell's house to examine the picture again. Wivell went, but was disgusted at finding that Mr. Liddell had gone out of town, and no one else keeping the engagement, he had his trouble for his pains.

THE DUNFORD PORTRAIT.

IN Great Newport Street, London, there formerly lived a print-seller named Dunford, who became the owner of this portrait about 1814. He purchased it from Edward Holder, a repairer of old paintings, for four guineas. Wivell ascertained that it was a forgery, and that it had been altered from a picture which Holder purchased for a few shillings. Holder's plan of altering pictures, as described by Kettle to Wivell, was by scraping off portions of the old painting with a knife, and then touching them up. A Mr. Hilder saw Holder at work on this very portrait, while it was being converted into one of Shakespeare. James Parry, an engraver, who lived in the same house with James Caulfield, (the latter possessing considerable knowledge of ancient portraits,) was present when Holder brought the picture (previous to its alteration) to Caulfield for his inspection. The latter, in Parry's presence, told Holder that it was a

The Dunford Portrait.

From Engraving by W. Sharp.

portrait of a Dutch Admiral, but that with some alterations, it "would make a very good Shakespeare."

W. Smith, a print-seller, stated that Holder brought the picture to him, and bought from him a couple of prints of Shakespeare.

When the picture was first altered, it was offered for sale to Mr. Kettle, for three pounds ten shillings. The offer was declined, and then Holder tried to sell it to Smith, but he also declined it. Caulfield was present when Holder brought it to the latter, and complimented the forger on his successful alteration. Subsequently Dunford purchased it for four pounds ten shillings; and while it was in his possession great numbers of people came to see it. Finally Dunford sold it for one hundred guineas to George Evans, Esq., of Beckenham, Kent. Considering that Dunford had only paid the forger four pounds ten shillings for it, this must be said to have been a very profitable sale to Dunford. Later it was sold at auction for forty guineas, at a sale of Evans' pictures, and purchased again by Dunford, under a commission given him by William Cattley, Esq.

Finally Wivell learned where Holder was living, and applied to him for information concerning this picture. In reply Holder wrote Wivell as follows:

"February 22nd, 1827.

"Sir:

"I have received your letter of the 19th instant, and in answer to your request, I will give every particular of the portrait I sold to Mr. Dunford, as a Shakespeare, (except the way by which I did it.)

"I bought the picture in New Turnstile, Holborn, for five shillings. It had been a large panel picture, of which this was the centre board, which I also reduced in order to make it more shapeable. I hung it up for some time in my painting room, as a study, for I admired it much. At last a thought came into my head, that it might be made into a Shakespeare, which I had never before attempted. Mr. Zincke, who then worked with me, approved of my plan, and I accordingly did so; without bestowing much time, as I did not intend to ask a large price. The body-garment was originally white, the earring, with other requisites, I put. When done, I added to it a frame; which I think cost me thirty shillings; and offered the whole to Mr. Dunford for five pounds. After he had looked at it for some time, he bid me four pounds ten shillings, which I accepted. Some few days after, Mr. Dunford came, and told me that I had sold him a great bargain, for which he would not take a thousand pounds. I was requested to call on him. I did so, and seeing him so very sanguine of his great bargain, I hoped he would not refuse a good offer when made, as I knew more about the picture than he imagined. To which he answered sharply, 'What, Sir, do you mean to say it is painted by yourself?' To which I made no reply. He again made answer, 'I did not know more about it than Mr. West or Sir T. Lawrence, and four hundred other competent judges, but that himself could not be deceived.' I found it was no use talking any more on the subject, so left him, with the observation, that they were blind altogether.

"I have not since then been able to see this picture, but judging from the print I do not perceive any good has been done by the analyzation it underwent, by my late beloved master, Mr. Hammond, whose abilities, in the art of repairing, was to the greatest perfection.

"It has since been said by Mr. Dunford to some of my friends, that he had made me a present of fifty pounds, but of which I have never received one shilling. I have never been inclined to dupe the world, as many have done in my situation of life; my object has ever been to sell my pictures cheap. I have a wife and nine children to support, and had I the advantages which others have made by my works, I should not be the poor man I now am. I am, Sir,

"Your most obedient humble servant,
"EDWARD HOLDER.
"*No. 3, Little Cambridge Street, Hackney Road.*

"N.B. I afterwards made another Shakespeare, which was worth a score such as the above. I sold it to Mr. Gwennap, in Brook Street, Grosvenor Square, for six pounds, which is the most I ever got for one. Mr. Gwennap questioned me if I had manufactured it, to which I answered in the affirmative; when he replied, had I asked him sixty pounds for it, he should have given it to me."*

As Holder's skill was doubted by Dunford, the former proceeded to make a portrait of a clergyman into one of Oliver Cromwell, which he sent by a messenger to Dunford. It was sold to him for four pounds, and was afterwards seen in Dunford's shop window, where it was doubtless much admired as a portrait of the Lord Protector! It is sad to think of a man, possessing the talent that Holder must have had, prostituting his abilities in this way. No doubt it was his poverty, and not his will, that consented.

The picture is unlike the other portraits of Shakespeare. The features are good—the nose being especially well done. The eyes have a serious expression, the hair is long and curling, the costume simple. A large, plain collar covers the shoulders completely, and has very small strings. The moustache is brushed up-

---

* *An Inquiry*, etc. London: 1827, 8vo., p. 182. It would be interesting to know what has become of Mr. Gwennap's picture.

wards, and a beard, which is light on the cheeks, covers the chin.

C. Turner engraved a large mezzotint, the size of life, from this portrait in 1815. Only two hundred and fifty copies were printed from this plate, which was then defaced. This has made the prints very rare.

The next year (1816), W. Sharp executed a beautiful plate, in his best manner, from the picture. It is surrounded by a neat frame, and is a very attractive print.

W. Holl next engraved the picture in 1827 for Wivell's *Inquiry*. It is very well done, and a good copy of Sharp's print, but not as fine as the latter.

In 1870 was published *Shakespeare and the Emblem Writers*, 8vo. This work was written by Henry Green, and on the title-page appears a small wood-cut, which bears a striking resemblance to Sharp's engraving of this portrait and Holl's copy of it. The beard is higher up on the cheek than in those engravings, but that may be the fault of the engraver of the wood-cut. It is stated that it is from an oil painting in the possession of Dr. Charles Clay, of Manchester, England. Can it be that Dr. Clay now possesses the Dunford portrait? Mr. Green does not give any pedigree of the picture.

THE WINSTANLEY PORTRAIT.

ON February 10, 1819, Thomas Winstanley, an auctioneer, of Liverpool, wrote a letter to *The Literary Gazette*, which was published February 20, 1819. In this he described a portrait of Shakespeare in his possession, which he stated he had purchased from a dealer, who had obtained it from a pawnbroker. Winstanley also said that a friend, whose opinion of a work of art was of much value, had pronounced it to be the work of Paul Vansomer; that it was in a fine state of preservation, and had the appearance of having been painted in Shakespeare's time.

Winstanley continues: "The picture shows only the head and a small part of the shoulders, the size of life. The dress is black, with a white collar thrown plain over the shoulders, and tied before with a cord and tassels. The portrait is under an arch, in the inside of which run the holly, the ivy, and the mistletoe. Under the portrait

THE WINSTANLEY PORTRAIT. 225

are two laurel leaves, on which are written, in old English characters, the following lines:

> "'As Holly, Ivie, Miseltoe defie the wintrye blast
> Despite of chillinge Envie, soe thy well earned fame shall laste
> Then lette the ever-living laurel beare
> Thy much loved name O Will. Shakspeare.
>
> "'B. I.'"

Ben Jonson could never have written this, and the duplication of the consonants is more than suspicious. But the forger of this portrait is known to have been W. F. Zincke, who made a business of altering pictures. He bought the picture originally from a Mr. Piercy. It then represented an elderly female, but Zincke altered her features into a semblance of Shakespeare. Having finished his alterations, he sold the picture to a pawnbroker named Benton, who in turn parted with it to a friend of Winstanley, and from him Winstanley obtained it.

It is said that four or five hundred pounds was the price asked for it by Winstanley, but no record of its sale has been preserved. An engraving from this picture, in outline, was published, with the four lines of "verse" given above.

THE ZINCKE PORTRAIT.

W. F. ZINCKE, an artist who seems to have vied with Edward Holder in the manufacture of spurious portraits of Shakespeare, was the painter of this picture.

The portrait is in an oval and shows the full face. The shape of the head, the arrangement of the hair and beard, all bear considerable resemblance to the Stratford bust, which Zincke appears to have taken as his model. On one side of the oval in which the picture is painted is a sketch of the poet with his dog and gun, and on the other side he is shown as a boy holding a horse—the latter being a representation of the story of his having followed that occupation while a youth.

Under one side of the oval is written "*Paynted by me, R. Bvrbage,*" and palm and oak leaves hang over the sides. On the back of the picture Zincke had pasted two pieces of paper, one purporting to contain some lines by

The Zincke Portrait.

From Engraving by W. Holl.

Ben Jonson, and the other the following: "Henry Spelman, Esq., the gyfte of John Selden, Esq., the 4th daye of May, 1640." The canvas was pieced in two places, and had been so treated as to look old, though quite new.

Zincke was a man of some ability, and had he applied his talents to an honest purpose might have produced good work. Wivell says that he purchased this picture of Zincke on account of the ingenuity displayed in it, and adds: "It is most pitiable to see an old man, for want of a more honest employment, obliged to have recourse to such means as fabricating portraits of Shakespeare, or otherwise starve."*

A capital engraving of it, by W. Holl, was published in 1827, in Wivell's *Inquiry*.

---

* *An Inquiry*, etc. London: 1827, 8vo. Supplement, p. 32.

THE TALMA PORTRAIT.

W. F. ZINCKE, who had already appeared as the fabricator of other spurious portraits of the poet, altered this one from another picture. It is on the wooden part of a pair of bellows, and Zincke concocted a wonderful story about a friend of his finding it in an old tavern. It was sold by one Foster to a Mr. Allen for a small sum. Foster told Wivell, in 1827, that he knew it was not an original portrait, and he had sold about thirty of "these mock original Shakespeares," and that he "never got more than six or eight guineas for the best, and I can assure you that I found it difficult to persuade many of the purchasers that they were not originals." Allen sold the picture to W. H. Ireland for eighty pounds. The condition of the sale, however, was that if there was any repainting or alteration on the picture it was to be returned to the seller. It was accordingly intrusted to a restorer and cleaner of pictures, a Mr. Ribet, who had no trouble in removing Zincke's paint, when an old lady with cap and blue ribbons appeared!

Ribet was employed to repair the picture, and soon made it a Shakespeare again. It was then taken to

France and sold to Talma, the actor, for a thousand francs. He had an elaborate case made for it of green morocco, lined with silk.

While in Talma's possession it was seen by a Mr. Brockedon, who informed its owner that Zincke had altered it into a portrait of Shakespeare. Talma had always believed that it was a genuine portrait of the poet, and was much disappointed to find that he was mistaken.

When Talma died this pair of bellows was sold, among his other effects, and brought three thousand one hundred francs. It is related that on one occasion Charles Lamb saw this picture, and fell down on his knees and kissed it!

As before stated, the portrait was on the wooden part of a pair of bellows. The following inscription, carved on the wood, was also on them:

"WHOM HAVE WE HERE
STUCKE ONNE THE BELLOWES?
THAT PRYNCE OF GOODE FELLOWES,
WILLIE SHAKSPERE.
OH! CURSTE UNTOWARDE LUCKE,
TO BE THUS MEANLIE STUCKE.
"POINS.

"NAYE, RATHER GLORIOUS LOTTE
TO HYMME ASSYGN'D,
WHO, LYKE TH' ALMIGHTIE RYDES
THE WYNGES OTH' WYNDE.
"PYSTOLLE."

THE MONUMENT IN WESTMINSTER ABBEY.

THE monument of Shakespeare in Westminster Abbey is from a design by W. Kent, and was executed by P. Scheemakers. It was erected in 1741. The funds required were raised by two performances given in the theatres, and the committee having the matter in charge consisted of the Earl of Burlington, Dr. Mead, Mr. Pope and Mr. Martin.

The poet is represented as leaning his right elbow on some books, which rest on a column. The head of the figure is somewhat like the Chandos portrait; the dress a doublet, knee breeches and cloak, which latter hangs from one shoulder. With his left hand he points to a scroll with an inscription on it from *The Tempest*. As a work of art it does not rank very high.

Several engravings have been made of this monument, the first by J. Maurer in 1742, the next by Miller in mezzotint. The latter is of folio size and very rare.

The Monument in Westminster Abbey.

FROM ENGRAVING BY B. HOLL.

About this time a large plate of the monument, by H. Gravelot, was published. This must not be confounded with a smaller plate by the same engraver which was published in Hanmer's Shakespeare, first edition, 1744, and again used in the second edition of his work, 1771. Both these engravings are well done, and accurately represent the monument.

Other plates by Dubose, Halpin, and Rothwell were also published; and a small engraving showing the iron railing around the monument was published in 1787 in Bell's Shakespeare, 16mo. The latter is very poor.

Finally, in 1827, Wivell published an excellent engraving of this pretentious monument in his *Inquiry*. It is by B. Holl and is very well done.

Photographs have also been taken, but owing to the position of the monument in the Abbey it is difficult to get a good light on the face, and they have not been very successful.

THE SHAKESPEARE GALLERY ALTO RELIEVO.

WHEN Boydell employed the best English artists of his day to paint the pictures which he afterward had engraved, he also caused to be made for the front of the Shakespeare Gallery, Pall Mall, London, a large monument in alto relievo, which was designed and executed by J. Banks, R.A.

Shakespeare is represented seated on a rock. He leans his left hand on the shoulder of an allegorical figure of a woman representing the Genius of Painting, who has a palette and brushes in one hand, while with the other she points to the poet as the best subject for her talent. The other allegorical figure is also a woman, who represents the Dramatic Genius, who is figured with a lyre, while she offers a wreath to the poet. The allegorical figures are well done, especially the Genius of Painting, whose figure is very graceful and charming,

The Shakespeare Gallery Alto=Relievo.

FROM ENGRAVING BY B. HOLL.

Der Evangelische Gallische Misa-Zeitung.

but the poet has not fared so well. The face has often been mistaken for George Washington, to whom the resemblance is striking.

The Alto Relievo was removed from London some years ago, and was presented by Mr. C. Holte Bracebridge to Shakespeare's Garden at New Place, Stratford-upon-Avon, where it now is. The stone from which the monument was cut is very soft, and owing to this unfortunate circumstance, it has suffered somewhat from exposure to the weather.*

A beautiful engraving of the Alto Relievo, of large folio size, was published by Boydell in 1798, as a frontispiece to his large series of illustrations of Shakespeare. It is engraved by James Stow. A smaller engraving by B. Smith was published in Boydell's edition of the poet's works. It is also very well done.

It was likewise engraved by Burnet Reading; Vitalba; S. Rawle, 1804; Girtin and Scriven, 1804, and by W. Humphry, 1826. A neat engraving of this group by B. Holl was published in 1827 in Wivell's *Inquiry*.

---

* This information was communicated by Samuel Timmins, Esq., J. P., to whom the present writer is indebted for this, and numberless other acts of kindness.

THE ROUBILIAC STATUE.

IN 1758 Lewis Francis Roubiliac sculptured this statue of Shakespeare for David Garrick. The latter, by his will, provided that it should go to the British Museum after the death of his wife, and it is now there.

It represents the poet leaning on a stand covered with drapery, in the act of composition. The face is taken from the Chandos portrait, and the costume is a doublet and knee breeches. Over all is thrown a loose cloak, which hangs from his shoulders.

Adrien Carpentiers painted a portrait of Roubiliac which represents him as finishing the model of this statue. This picture was engraved by D. Martin in 1765, and an excellent plate of the same portrait by W. Holl was published in Wivell's *Inquiry*, 1827.

The Roubiliac Statue.

From Engraving by W. Holl.

The Ward Statue.

From Photograph of Original by Rockwood.

THE WARD STATUE.

THIS statue, which is the work of Mr. J. Q. A. Ward, was erected in Central Park, New York, May 23, 1872. In modelling the head Mr. Ward has closely followed the Stratford bust, but he has given the face a much more intellectual expression than appears in that effigy. The cheeks are thinner and the face more refined, and yet one can see at a glance that the Stratford bust has been the model.

The poet is represented standing, as if lost in thought. He holds a book in his right hand and has his finger between the leaves to keep the place where he has been reading. The left hand rests on the hip, and the head is inclined slightly forward. The costume consists of doublet and hose, with puffed-out breeches, and a cloak hanging from the left shoulder, and is very graceful and well conceived.

The statue is larger than life and is made of bronze. It has been admirably photographed by Rockwood, of New York; and a poor and spiritless wood engraving of it, by Davis, appeared in *The Aldine* in 1872.

INDEX

INDEX.

ADLARD, H., his engraving of Marshall's copy of the Droeshout, 66.
Adolphus, Gustavus, 93, 99.
Agar, his engraving of the Hilliard miniature, 184, 186.
    I. S., his engraving of the Stratford bust, 40.
Albert Hall, 191, 210.
Allen, bought the Talma portrait, and sold it to W. H. Ireland, 228.
Alto Relievo, the Shakespeare Gallery, 232.
Amsterdam, 102, 103, 122, 123, 124.
Anecdotes of Painting, Walpole's, 123.
Anne, effigy of, 111.
Apostool, C., his engraving of the Chandos portrait, 87.
Archæological Association, visit of the, to see the Stratford portrait, 156.
Arlaud, B., his drawing of the Chandos portrait, 83.
Armstrong, Cosmo, his engraving of the Felton portrait, 151.

Artlett, R. A., his engraving of the Chandos portrait, 92.
Art Museum, Boston, 197.
Arundel Society, its photograph of the Chandos portrait, 78, 79, 80.
    Its photograph of the Hampton Court portrait, 181.
Ashborne portrait, 166.
    Compared with the Jansen portrait, 169.
    Description of the, 169.
    G. F. Storm's mezzotint of the, 170.
    Its history amounts to nothing, 169.
Ashby, R., his engraving of the Stratford bust, 39.
Athenæum, The, 159, 160.
    Article on the Chandos portrait, 73, 74.
Audinet, his engraving of the Chandos portrait, 86.
Auriol, Charles, 189.
Auriol miniature, 190.

BACON, Sir Francis, search for his body, 13.
Banks, J., designed and executed the Shakespeare Gallery Alto Relievo, 232.
Barnes, J., 177.
Barry, Mrs., her purchase of the Chandos portrait, 69.
Battersea, 189.
Bayeux, Bishop of, his tomb opened, 4.
Becker, Dr. Ernst, now has the Death Mask, 112.
Becker, Ludwig, his account of the discovery of the Death Mask, 96.
  Death of, 112.
  Mentioned, 94, 95, 96, 98, 101.
  Went to England, 112.
  Went to Melbourne, 112.
Bell, John, thought that the Stratford bust was from a mask, 33.
Bell, R.C., his engraving of the Droeshout, 65.
Ben Jonson, 11, 19, 46, 50, 51, 101, 102, 172, 214, 225.
  His grave examined, 11.
Bennett, S., his engraving of the Chandos portrait, 87.
Benton, originally owned the Winstanley portrait, 225.
Berg, Hermann, his drawing of the Chandos portrait, 92.
Betterton, his purchase of the Chandos portrait, 69, 71.
Birmingham Archæological Association, visit of the, to see the Stratford portrait, 156.

Birrell, A., his engraving of the Stratford bust, 38.
Blackfriars, 124.
Bloomsbury, 208.
Blount, Mountjoy, his portrait engraved by Droeshout, 47.
Boaden, J., his drawing of the Stratford bust, 40.
  His search for the Jansen portrait, 130.
  On the Chandos portrait, 81.
  On the Droeshout engraving, 48.
  On the Felton portrait, 146.
  On the Hilliard miniature, 184.
  On the Jansen portrait, 132.
  On the John Wilson Croker copy of the Jansen portrait, 134.
  On the Stratford bust, 29.
  On the Zoust portrait, 202.
  Saw the Zucchero portrait at R. Cosway's, 204.
  Says that *Ut magus* is on the Jansen portrait, 133.
  Thought that the Zucchero portrait resembled Torquato Tasso, 205.
Boardman miniature, 206.
  Called the Norwich portrait, 207.
  Costume of the, resembles that of the Chandos portrait, 207.
  Description of the, 206.
  Fisk offered five hundred pounds for the, 207.
  History of the, 207.
  Inscription on the, 206.

INDEX.

Boardman miniature, in the possession of G. W. W. Firth, 206.
   Izard owned the, 207.
   Moustache of the, like that of the Stratford bust, 207.
Boardman, R. R., was long the owner of the Boardman miniature, 207.
Bohn, on the Droeshout engraving, 47.
Booth, 203.
Booth, Lionel, had a copy of the Zoust portrait, 203.
Boston Art Museum portrait, 196.
   Description of the, 198.
   Its history, 196.
   Sonrel's photographs of the, 197, 198.
Boswell, James, 182, 183.
   On the Felton portrait, 145.
Boydell, 232, 233.
Boydell, J., his drawing of the Stratford bust, 38.
Boydell, Josiah, his copy of the Felton portrait, 147.
   Made a copy of the Felton portrait for George Steevens, 145.
Bracebridge, C. Holte, presented the Shakespeare Gallery Alto Relievo to Shakespeare's Garden, New Place, 233.
British Museum, 111, 112, 113.
Britton, John, induced George Bullock to make a cast of the Stratford bust, 33.
   On the Droeshout engraving, 48.
Brocas, H., his engraving of the Droeshout, 60.

Brook Street, 222.
Brooks, Vincent, his chromo-lithograph of the Lumley portrait, 195.
Bryant, 216, 217.
   Owned the Liddell portrait before it was forged by Holder, 216.
Buckingham, Duke of, 69.
Buckingham, Duchess of, 69, 70.
Buckland, Frank, account of his efforts to examine Ben Jonson's skull, 11.
Bullock, George, made a cast of the Stratford bust, 33.
Burbage, Richard, 68, 70, 72.
   His portrait at Dulwich College, 72.
Burdett Coutts, Baroness, the Lumley portrait purchased by, 193.
Burges, Sir James Bland, 182, 183.
Burlington House, 191.
Burn, George Adam, 191.
Burn portrait, 191.
   Description of the, 191.
   Has no history, 191.
   Resemblance of, to the Stratford bust, 191.
Burney, his drawing of the Chandos portrait, 87.
Burns, Robert, his body examined, 11.

CAERNARVON, Marquis of, 69, 70.
   Capell, his *Notes and Various Readings*, 126.
Cardinal Wolsey, 179.

Carus, 111.
Cattley, William, 219.
Caulfield, James, 218, 219.
Central Park, 235.
Cervantes, age of when he died, 119.
    Death of, 118.
    Description of appearance of, 118.
    The Death Mask, suggested as representing, 118.
Challis portrait, 199.
    Description of the, 199.
    Friswell on the, 199.
    Has no history, 199.
    Its resemblance to the Death Mask, 200.
Challis, Thomas, 199.
Chandos, Duke of, 69, 70.
Chandos portrait, 67, 119, 127, 175, 177, 178, 193, 194, 195, 200, 203.
    Apostool's engraving of the, 87.
    Arundel Society's photograph of the, 78, 79, 80.
    Audinet's engraving of the, 86.
    B. Arlaud's drawing of the, 83.
    B. Holl's engraving of the, 89, 90.
    Betterton's purchase of the, 69, 71.
    Boaden on the, 81.
    Burney's drawing of the, 87.
    C. Knight's engraving of the, 85.
    Dean's engraving of the, 88.
    Description of the, 74.
    Dr. C. M. Ingleby on the, 79.
    Edward Smith's engraving of the, 89.

Chandos portrait, E. Scriven's engraving of the, 90.
    Frank Jones' chromo-lithograph of the, 92.
    Freeman's engraving of the, 89.
    Friswell on the, 81.
    Fry's engraving of the, 87.
    G. Dalziel's engraving of the, 91.
    G. Duchange's engraving of the, 83.
    G. Greatbach's engraving of the, 91.
    George Scharf on the, 75, 80.
    Goldar's engraving of the, 85.
    G. Vander Gucht's engraving of the, 84, 86.
    G. Vertue's engraving of the, 83, 84.
    Heath's engraving of the, 88.
    Hermann Berg's drawing of the, 92.
    H. Gravelot's engraving of the, 84.
    Holl's engraving of the, 86.
    Hollis' engraving of the, 90.
    Houbraken's engraving of the, 84.
    H. Robinson's engraving of the, 89.
    H. Rodd on the, 76.
    Its pedigree not capable of proof, 71.
    James Faed's engraving of the, 92.
    John Cochran's engraving of the, 89.
    John Faed's painting of the, 91.
    John Hall's engraving of the, 85.
    John Payne Collier on the, 72.
    John Thompson's engraving of the, 88.
    Le Goux's engraving of the, 86.
    Lud. du Guernier's engraving of the, 83.

INDEX. 243

Chandos portrait, more like the Stratford bust than the Droeshout engraving, 80.
   Mrs. Barry's purchase of the, 69.
   M. Vander Gucht's engraving of the, 82.
   Nicoll, Nicholl, or Nicholls' ownership of the, 69, 70, 73.
   N. Parr's engraving of the, 86.
   Oldy's notes to Langbaine, on the, 73.
   Ozias Humphry's drawing of the, 77.
   Preston's photograph of the, 92.
   P. Rohrbach's lithograph of the, 92.
   P. W. Tomkins' engraving of the, 87.
   R. A. Artlett's engraving of the, 92.
   Resemblance of the Lumley portrait to the, 194.
   R. Corbould's drawing of the, 87.
   Robert Keck's purchase of the, 69, 70.
   Samuel Cousins' mezzotint of the, 79, 90.
   S. Bennett's engraving of the, 87.
   Scriven's engraving of the, 88.
   S. Freeman's engraving of the, 90.
   S. Harding's drawing of the, 86.
   Sir Joshua Reynolds on the, 75.
   Sir Joshua Reynolds said to have made a copy of the, 72.
   Steevens on the, 77.
   Supposed to represent Shakespeare as Shylock, 82.
   T. Cook's engraving of the, 85.
   T. D. Scott's drawing of the, 91.
Chandos portrait, *The Athenæum* article on the, 73, 74.
   The best known of all the portraits of Shakespeare, 67.
   The costume of the Boardman miniature resembles it, 207.
   The face of the Roubiliac statue somewhat like the, 234.
   The Hampton Court portrait resembles it somewhat, 180.
   Vander Gucht's drawing of the, 130.
   W. Harvey's drawing of the, 88.
   W. Holl's engraving of the, 89.
   William Page on the, 78.
   Wivell's drawing of the, 88, 89.
Chantrey, Sir Francis, thought that the Stratford bust was from a mask, 33.
Charlecote Hall, 124.
Charles I., 178, 179.
   His body examined, 8.
Charles II., 172, 173, 180.
Charles Street, 216.
Chaucer, 194.
Chauvel, 149.
Chelsea, 125.
Chetwin, P., 173.
Chromo-lithograph, by Vincent Brooks, of the Lumley portrait, 195.
Chromo-phototype, New Shakespeare Society's of the Stratford bust, 44.
Clay, Dr. Charles, supposed to now own the Dunford portrait, 223.
Clift, William, 174, 175, 176.

244 INDEX.

Clopton, Edward, 155.
Clopton House, the Stratford portrait purchased at a sale at the, 153.
Clopton, Sir Hugh, 155.
Cochran, John, his engraving of the Chandos portrait, 89.
    His engraving of the Felton portrait, 152.
College of Surgeons, 174, 176.
Collier, John Payne, his paper on the Chandos portrait, 72.
Collins, Simon, cleaned off the white paint from the Stratford bust, 26.
    Cleaned the Stratford portrait, 153.
    His photographs of the Stratford portrait, 163.
    Mentioned, 153, 154, 156, 157, 159, 162, 163.
Collyer, J., his engraving of the Felton portrait, 151.
Cologne, 93, 94, 99, 112.
Combe, John, 22.
Condell, Henry, 45.
Cook, H., his engraving of the Droeshout, 62.
Cook, T., his engraving of the Chandos portrait, 85.
Cooper, R., his engraving of Croker's copy of the Jansen portrait, 134.
    His engraving of the Jansen portrait, 137.
    His engraving of the Stace portrait, 209.
Copeland, 173.

Corbould, R., his drawing of the Chandos portrait, 87.
Cosway, R., could not give Boaden any information concerning the Zucchero portrait, 205.
    Owned the Zucchero portrait, 204.
Cousins, Samuel, his mezzotint of the Chandos portrait, 79, 90.
Critical Review, the, 127, 128.
Croker, John Wilson, the discovery of his copy of the Jansen portrait, 135.
    His copy of the Jansen portrait, 134.
Cromwell, Oliver, 179.
    Appearance of the eye in Mask of, 115.
    Effigy of, 111.
    His portrait manufactured out of a clergyman's by Holder, 222.
Crystal Palace, 175.
Curzon, Penn Asheton, 130.

DALLAWAY, 124, 125.
    Dalziel, G., his engraving of the Chandos portrait, 91.
Darmstadt, 94, 112, 113, 119.
D'Avenant, Sir William, 68, 69, 70, 172, 173, 178.
    His edition of *Macbeth*, 173.
Davenport, Rev. Dr., 33.
Davis, his engraving of the Ward statue, 235.
Dead, features and clothing of, often preserved, 3.

INDEX. 245

Dean, his engraving of the Chandos portrait, 88.
Dean, T. A., his engraving of the Stratford bust, 40.
Death Mask, 93, 177, 200.
    Comparison of, with the Stratford bust, 116.
    Crayon drawing of Page's bust, from the, 120.
    Discovery of the, 96, 97.
    Friswell on the appearance of the left eye of the, 115.
    Friswell thinks that the Kesselstadt picture is a copy from the, 101.
    Hairs on the, 104, 105.
    Healthy appearance of the, 115.
    Inscription on back of the, 97, 108.
    Is in a fair state of preservation, 107.
    J. Niessen's portrait from the, 121.
    Lines cut in the moustache and goatee of the, 107.
    Photographs of the, 121.
    Resemblance of the Duke of Devonshire bust to the, 177.
    The Jansen portrait more nearly resembles it than any other, 133.
    The price asked for the, 113.
    William Page's bust from the, 120.
    William Page had the greatest faith in the, 119.
    William Page made masks from the, 119.
Death Mask, William Page on the appearance of the left eye in the, 115.
    William Page's portrait from the, 121.
    W. J. Thoms suggested that it represented Cervantes, 118.
Delattre, his engraving of Marshall's copy of the Droeshout, 66.
Digges, L., lines on Shakespeare, 23.
D'Lisles, 179.
Douglas, William, 201.
Dramatic Genius, 232.
Droeshout engraving, 45, 119, 141, 147, 200.
    Augustus Fox's engraving of, 62.
    Boaden on the, 48.
    Bohn on the, 47.
    Cannot be successfully copied on wood, 63.
    C. Picart's engraving of the, 62.
    Dr. Ingleby on the, 49.
    Engravers have tried to improve the, 59.
    Friswell on the, 49.
    F. W. Fairbolt on the Halliwell-Phillipps copy of the, 53.
    George Steevens on the, 48.
    H. Brocas' engraving of the, 60.
    H. Cook's engraving of the, 62.
    Heliotypes of the, 65.
    H. Robinson's engraving of the, 63.
    Its merits discussed, 50.
    J. O. Halliwell-Phillipps' copy of the, 52.

Droeshout engraving, J. O. Halliwell-Phillipps on the, 50.
John Britton on the, 48.
J. Swaine's engraving of the, 61.
Lenox on the Halliwell-Phillipps copy of the, 57.
Lines on the, 46.
Marshall's copy of the, 59.
Opinions of critics on the merits of, have been various, 47.
Photographs of, not generally successful, 64.
Photographs of the, 64, 65.
Photo-lithographic copies of the, 64, 65.
Photo-zincographic copy of, 64.
Probably from a painting, 51.
R. C. Bell's engraving of the, 65.
Rivers' engraving of the, 61.
R. Sawyer's engraving of the, 61.
Samuel Ireland's engraving of the, 61.
Steevens believed that it was from the Felton portrait, 51.
Steevens on the, 141.
Supposed to represent Shakespeare in a theatrical costume, 51.
The copy of, in Bell's edition of Shakespeare, 60.
The copy of, in Forster's *Few Remarks*, etc., 63.
The copy of, in Grant White's edition of Shakespeare, 63.
The copy of, in Johnson and Steevens' edition of Shakespeare, 1778, 60.
Droeshout engraving, the copy of, in Knight's Cabinet edition of Shakespeare, 63.
The copy of, in Mary Cowden Clarke's edition of Shakespeare, 65.
The copy of, in *The Legend of Shakespeare's Crab Tree*, 63.
The copy of, in the reprint of the First Folio, 1807, 61.
The copy of, published about 1827 by W. Smith, 62.
The differences between J. O. Halliwell-Phillipps' copy of, and the ordinary impressions, 52.
The Felton portrait not the original of the, 51.
Thurston's drawing of the, 61.
Unlike the Stratford bust, 19.
W. Fairthorne's engraving of the, 59.
W. H. Worthington's engraving of the, 62.
William Page on the Halliwell-Phillipps copy of the, 55.
William Smith on the Halliwell-Phillipps copy of the, 54.
Wivell on the, 48.
W. J. Linton's engraving of the, 63.
Wood-cuts of the, 63, 66.
W. Sherwin's engraving of the, 60.
Droeshout, Martin, the faults of his engraving, 51.
The various portraits engraved by him, 47.

INDEX.

Dryden, his verses on the copy of the Chandos portrait sent to him by Kneller, 71.
Dubose, his engraving of the Monument in Westminster Abbey, 231.
Duchange, G., his engraving of the Chandos portrait, 83.
Duke of Buckingham, 175.
Duke of Devonshire, 175, 177.
Duke of Hamilton, 130, 131.
Duke of Somerset, 130, 168.
Duke of York, 172.
Duke of Devonshire bust, 172.
    Discovery of the, 174, 176.
    Its purchase by the Duke of Devonshire, 175, 176.
    Its resemblance to the Death Mask, 177.
Dugdale, his *Life, Diary*, etc., 22.
Du Guernier, Lud., his engraving of the Chandos portrait, 83.
Duke's Theatre, the, 172, 173, 175, 176.
Dulwich College, 68, 72.
Dulwich Gallery, picture of Ben Jonson in the, 102.
Dunkarton, R., his engraving of the Jansen portrait, 131, 136.
Dunford, 218, 219, 220, 221, 222.
Dunford portrait, 218.
    C. Turner's mezzotint of, 223.
    Description of the, 222.
    Formerly a Dutch Admiral, 219.
    History of the, 218.

Dunford portrait, supposed engraving of, in Green's *Shakespeare and the Emblem Writers*, 223.
    W. Holl's engraving of the, 223.
    W. Sharp's engraving of the, 223.
Dürer, Albrecht, 93, 99.

EARL of Scarborough, 192.
    Earl of Southampton, 124.
Earlom, R., his mezzotint of the Jansen portrait, 126, 127, 130, 136.
    His mezzotint of the Jansen portrait, *Ut magus*, above the, 133.
Ear-rings, Englishmen of Shakespeare's day wore them, 80.
Eastcheap, the great fire which destroyed it in 1666, 143.
Edward IV., his tomb opened, 5.
Edward VI., 179.
Effigies, ancient, Dr. Schaaffhausen on, 111.
Effigy of Anne, 111.
    Of Cromwell, 111.
    Of James I., 111.
    Of King Edward VI., 111.
    Of King William, 111.
    Of Nelson, 111.
    Of Queen Elizabeth, 111.
    Of Queen Mary, 111.
Eginton, F., his engraving of the Stratford bust, 38.
Egyptian mummies, 111.
Elizabeth, Queen, her portrait painted by Zucchero, 204.

248 INDEX.

Ellesmere, Earl of, 70, 79.
Ellesmere, Lord, 145.
Elze, Karl, 102.
Every Man in his Humour, 51.
Examiner, The, on the Stratford portrait, 161.
Exhibition of the Industry of All Nations, 193.

FAED, James, his engraving of the Chandos portrait, 92.
Faed, John, his painting of the Chandos portrait, 91.
Fairholt, F. W., his drawing of the Stratford bust, 32.
   His engraving of Stratford bust, 41.
   On the Halliwell-Phillipps copy of the Droeshout engraving, 53.
   On the Stratford bust, 32.
Fairfax, William, his portrait engraved by Droeshout, 47.
Fairthorne, W., his engraving of the Droeshout, 59.
Felton portrait, 141.
   A. Wivell's engraving of the, 152.
   Boaden on the, 146.
   Cosmo Armstrong's engraving of the, 151.
   C. Warren's engravings of the, 150.
   First shown to George Steevens, 141.
   H. Wright Smith's engraving of the, 152.

Felton portrait, inscription on the back of the, 146.
   Is well drawn and colored, 147.
   I. Thomson's engraving of the, 150.
   J. Cochran's engraving of the, 152.
   J. Collyer's engraving of the, 151.
   J. Godfrey's engraving of the, 149.
   J. Neagle's engraving of the, 150.
   John Thurston's drawing of the, 150.
   Josiah Boydell's copy of the, owned by Harris, 147.
   J. Wilson's account of the history of the, 142.
   J. Wilson's account of, to George Steevens, 143.
   Offered for sale in 1870, 145.
   Owned by Westmacott, 145.
   Richardson's proposal for the publication of the engravings of the, 149.
   S. Felton's purchase of the, 142.
   S. Felton sold it to G. Nichol for forty guineas, 144.
   The Droeshout engraving probably not from the, 51.
   The panel on which it is painted is split, 146.
   T. Trotter's engravings of the, 148, 149.
   W. Holl's engraving of the, 151.
   Wivell on the, 147.
   W. T. Fry's engraving of the, 151.
Felton, S., 141.
   His purchase of the Felton portrait, 142.

INDEX.

Felton, S., sold the Felton portrait to G. Nichol for forty guineas, 144.

Finden, W., his engraving of the Stratford bust, 39.

Fire, the great, which destroyed Eastcheap in 1666, 143.

Firth, G. W. W., has the Boardman miniature in his possession, 206.

Fisk, offered five hundred pounds for the Boardman miniature, 207.

Fitzwilliam, Earl, owned Dryden's copy of the Chandos portrait, 72.

Folio, First, 45, 49, 56, 203.
    Fourth, 45, 46.
    Second, 45.
    Third, 45, 46.

Foster, sold the Talma portrait, 228.

Fox, Augustus, his engraving of the Droeshout, 62.

Fox, John, his portrait engraved by Droeshout, 47.

Freeman, his engraving of the Chandos portrait, 89.

Freeman, S., his engraving of the Chandos portrait, 90.

Friswell, J. Hain, his comparison of the Death Mask and the Stratford bust, 116.
    On the appearance of the left eye of the Death Mask, 115.
    On the Challis portrait, 199.
    On the Chandos portrait, 81.
    On the Droeshout engraving, 49.

Friswell, J. Hain, on the O'Connell portrait, 210.
    On the Stratford bust, 28.
    Repeats Boaden's statement that *Ut magus* is on the Jansen portrait, 134.
    Thinks that the Kesselstadt picture is a copy of the Death Mask, 101.

Fry, his engraving of the Chandos portrait, 87.
    His engraving of the Stratford bust, 40.

Fry, W. T., his engraving of the Felton portrait, 151.
    His engraving of the Stratford bust, 39.

GARDNER, his engraving of the Jansen portrait, 136.

Garrard, Mark, claimed to have painted the O'Connell portrait, 210.

Garrick Club, 175, 176, 177, 178.

Garrick, David, 202.
    Inaugurated a jubilee at Stratford in 1769, 158.
    The Roubiliac statue made for, 234.

Genius of Painting, 232.

Gilliland portrait, 211.
    Description of the, 211.
    Different from all the other portraits, 211.
    History of the, 211.
    Owned by Thomas Gilliland, 211.
    W. Holl's engraving of the, 212.

Gilliland, Thomas, owned the Gilliland portrait, 211.
Girtin and Scriven, their engraving of the Shakespeare Gallery Alto Relievo, 233.
Globe Theatre, 196.
Godfrey, J., his engraving of the Felton portrait, 149.
Goldar, his engraving of the Chandos portrait, 85.
Golden Chamber of the Ursula Church, 112.
Gopsal, 126, 130.
Graham, John, 208.
Grave, proposition to open Shakespeare's, 1.
Gravelot, H., his engraving of the Chandos portrait, 84.
    His engravings of the Monument in Westminster Abbey, 231.
    His engraving of Vertue's plate of the Stratford bust, 37.
Greatbach, G., his engraving of the Chandos portrait, 91.
    His engraving of the Jansen portrait, 139.
    His engraving of Stratford bust, 41.
Great Newport Street, 218.
    Ormond Street, 129, 216.
    Queen Street, 208.
Green, Henry, his mezzotint of the Zucchero portrait, 205.
    Shakespeare and the Emblem Writers, 223.
Grenville, 154.

Grignion, his engraving of the Stratford bust, 38.
Grosvenor Square, 222.
Gwennap, his portrait of Shakespeare, sold to him by Holder, 222.

HACKNEY Road, 221.
    Hair, change of color of, when cut off, 105.
Hairs affixed to the Death Mask, 104, 105.
Halpin, his engraving of the Monument in Westminster Abbey, 231.
Hammond, 221.
Hardie, Dr., owned the Hardie portrait, 213.
Hardie portrait, 213.
    Description of the, 213.
    Forged by Zincke, 213.
    Inscriptions on the, 213, 214.
    Owned by Dr. Hardie, 213.
    Resembled the Stratford bust, 214.
Halford, Sir Henry, his account of the examination of Charles I.'s body, 8.
Hall, John, his engravings of the Chandos portrait, 85.
    His grave, 2.
Hall, Dr. John, 50.
Hall, Susanna, her grave, 2.
Halliwell-Phillipps, J. O., his copy of the Droeshout engraving, 52.
    On Shakespeare's skull, 14.
    On the Droeshout engraving, 50.

INDEX.   251

Halliwell-Phillipps, J. O., on the restoration of the Stratford bust, 27.
   On the Stratford bust, 27.
   On the Stratford portrait, 160.
Hamilton, Duke of, 130, 131.
Hampton Court Palace, 179.
Hampton Court portrait, 179.
   Arundel Society's photograph of the, 181.
   Description of the, 180.
   Its history, 179.
   More like the Chandos portrait than any other, 180.
Hardiknutian tablet, 145.
Harding, S., his drawing of the Chandos portrait, 86.
   His drawing of the Stratford bust, 38.
Hare, James, his account of Shakespeare's grave, 15.
Harland, T. W., his engraving of the Hilliard miniature, 186.
Harris, bought J. Boydell's copy of the Felton portrait, 148.
   Owned J. Boydell's copy of the Felton portrait, 147.
Hart, Prof. John S., 113.
Harvey, W., his drawing of the Chandos portrait, 88.
Heath, his engraving of the Chandos portrait, 88.
Heliotypes of the Droeshout engraving, 65.
Heminge, John, 45.
Henry VIII., 179.

Henry VIII., his remains examined, 6, 8.
Hermetically sealed coffin, Shakespeare probably buried in one, 3.
Hilder, 218.
Hilliard miniature, 182.
   Agar's engraving of the, 184, 186.
   B. Holl's engraving of the, 186.
   Boaden on the, 184.
   Description of the, 185.
   History of the, 182.
   T. W. Harland's engraving of the, 186.
Hilliard, Nicholas, 184.
Historia Naturalis, 109.
Hobbs, 154.
Holbein, 180.
Holborn, 220.
Holder, Edward, 215, 216, 217, 218, 219, 221, 222, 226.
   Dunford purchased the Dunford portrait from, 218.
   Forged the Liddell portrait, 215.
   His account of how he altered the Dunford portrait, 220.
   His plan of altering portraits, 218.
   Sold the Dunford portrait to Dunford for four pounds ten shillings, 220.
Holl, B., his engravings of the Chandos portrait, 89, 90.
   His engraving of the Hilliard miniature, 186.
   His engraving of the Monument in Westminster Abbey, 231.

252   INDEX.

Holl, B., his engraving of the Shakespeare Gallery Alto Relievo, 233.
Holl, Francis, his engraving of the Stratford bust, 42.
Holl, W., his engraving of the Chandos portrait, 89.
    His engraving of the Dunford portrait, 223.
    His engraving of the Felton portrait, 151.
    His engraving of the Gilliland portrait, 212.
    His engraving of the Jennings miniature, 190.
    His engraving of the Roubiliac statue, 234.
    His engraving of the Stace portrait, 209.
    His engraving of the Zincke portrait, 227.
    His engraving of the Zoust portrait, 203.
    His engraving of the Zucchero portrait, 205.
Hollis, his engraving of the Chandos portrait, 90.
Holy Trinity Church, 2, 21.
Hopwood, his engraving of the Jansen portrait, 139.
Houbraken, his engraving of the Chandos portrait, 84.
Howarth, 197, 198.
Howe, Emmanuel Scroope, 132.

Howson, John, his portrait engraved by Droeshout, 47.
Hughes, Margaret, 132.
Humphry, Ozias, his drawing of the Chandos portrait for Malone, 77.
Humphry, W., his engraving of the Shakespeare Gallery Alto Relievo, 233.
Hunt, William Oakes, 153, 154, 159, 162.
    Owned the Stratford portrait, 153.
    Presented the Stratford portrait to the town of Stratford, 162.

IMMERZEEL, *Levens en Werken der Hollandsche Kunstschilders*, 123.
Indentation over the right eyebrow of the Death Mask, 113.
Ingleby, Dr. C. M., his efforts to obtain a correct photograph of the Stratford portrait, 163.
    His *Shakespeare's Bones*, 2.
    In favor of opening Shakespeare's grave, 2.
    On the Chandos portrait, 79.
    On the Droeshout engraving, 49.
    On the Stratford bust, 29.
Inscription on the back of the Death Mask, 97, 108.
    On the back of the Felton portrait, 146.
    On the Boardman miniature, 206.
    On the fire-proof safe in which the Stratford portrait is kept, 163.
    On the Hardie portrait, 213, 214.

Inscription on the Talma portrait, 229.
    Under the Stratford bust, 24.
    Under the Winstanley portrait, 225.
Ireland, Samuel, his drawing of the Droeshout, 61.
    His drawing of the Stratford bust, 38.
Ireland, W. H., formerly owned the Talma portrait, 228.
Izard, owned the Boardman miniature, 207.

JAMES I., 83, 180, 185.
    Effigy of, 111.
    Vertue's engraving of, 128.
James, Duke of York, 172.
Jannsen (Jansen), 122.
Jannsens (Jansen), 122.
Jansen, Cornelius, 73, 75, 126, 127, 132.
    His name also spelled Jannsen, Jannsens and Johnson, 122.
    Malone's statement regarding the arrival of, in England, 125.
    Price of his pictures, 124.
    The date of his first works in England, 123.
Jansen portrait, 122.
    Boaden on John Wilson Croker's copy of the, 134.
    Boaden on the, 132.
    Boaden's search for the, 130.
    Compared with the Ashborne portrait, 169.
    Earlom's mezzotint of the, 130, 136.

Jansen portrait, Gardner's engraving of the, 136.
    G. Greatbach's engraving of the, 139.
    Given by the Duke of Hamilton to the Duke of Somerset, 130.
    Hopwood's engraving of the, 139.
    H. Robinson's engraving of the, 138.
    In the possession of the Duke of Hamilton in 1811, 131.
    John Wilson Croker's copy of the, 134.
    J. R. Jobbins' lithograph of the, 139.
    Lacour's engraving of the, 139.
    More nearly resembles the Death Mask than any other, 133.
    Not an authentic picture of Shakespeare, 122.
    Not known who painted it, 122.
    Page's engraving of the, 138.
    Photograph of Charles Turner's mezzotint of the, 138.
    R. Cooper's engraving of Croker's copy of the, 137.
    R. Cooper's engraving of the, 137.
    R. Dunkarton's engraving of the, 131, 136.
    R. Earlom's mezzotint of the, 126.
    R. Page's engraving of the, 137.
    Sometimes called the Somerset, 122.
    The panel on which it is painted is split in two places, 133.
    T. Wright's engraving of the, 138.
Jennens, Charles, 126, 127, 128, 129, 130, 132, 134.

254 INDEX.

Jennens, Charles, defence of his *King Lear*, 128.
    His death, 130.
    His edition of *King Lear*, 126, 127, 128.
    His house at Gopsal, 126.
    Review of his edition of *King Lear*, 127.
Jennings, H. Constantine, 189.
Jennings miniature, 189.
    History of the, 189.
    W. Holl's engraving of the, 190.
    Wilson on the, 190.
    Wivell on the, 190.
Jobbins, J. R., his lithograph of the Jansen portrait, 139.
Johnson, Gerard, 18, 21, 103, 157.
Johnson (Jansen), 122.
Jones, Frank, his chromo-lithograph of the Chandos portrait, 92.
Jonson, Ben, 11, 19, 46, 50, 51, 101, 102, 172, 214.
    His grave examined, 11.
    His lines on the Droeshout engraving, 46.
    Picture of, in Dulwich Gallery, 102.
    The Kesselstadt picture supposed to represent him, 101, 102, 104.
Jourdan, S., 94, 101.
Joy, Abby, 197.
Joy, Benjamin, 196.
Jubilee at Stratford-upon-Avon, 158.

KECK, Robert, his purchase of the Chandos portrait, 69, 70.
Kesselstadt picture, 94, 95, 96, 97, 98, 99, 100, 101, 102, 104.
    Supposed to represent Ben Jonson, 101, 102, 104.
Kettle, 218, 219.
Kingston, Clements, 166, 168.
    His letter to Wivell, 166.
King Lear, Charles Jennens' defence of his edition of, 128.
    Jennens' edition of, 126.
Kneller, Sir Godfrey, 67, 71, 180.
    His copy of the Chandos portrait, 67.
    Verses sent by Dryden to, 71.
Knight, C., his engraving of the Chandos portrait, 85.

LACOUR, his engraving of the Jansen portrait, 139.
Lamb, Charles, said to have fallen on his knees before the Talma portrait, and to have kissed it, 229.
Langbaine, Oldy's notes on, on the Chandos portrait, 73.
Laurel Street, 210.
Lawford Church, graves opened at, 3.
Lawrence, Sir Thomas, 184, 221.
Lear, King, Charles Jennens' defence of his edition of, 128.
Le Goux, his engraving of the Chandos portrait, 86.

Leicester, Lord, 144.
Lely, 180.
Lenox, on the Halliwell-Phillipps copy of the Droeshout engraving, 57.
Liddell portrait, 215.
    Owned by Bryant, before it was forged by Holder, 216.
    Owned by Thomas Liddell, 215.
    Wivell discovered that Holder forged it, 215.
Liddell, Thomas, 217.
Lip, upper, length of, in Stratford bust, 33.
Lincoln's Inn Fields, 172, 176.
Lines over Shakespeare's grave, 17.
Linnell, 208.
Linton, W. J., his engraving of Stratford bust, 42.
    His engraving of the Droeshout, 63.
Little Cambridge Street, 221.
London and its Environs, 129.
Lord Ellesmere, 145.
Lord Leicester, 144.
Lord Lumley, 192, 194.
Lord Orford, 144.
Lord Spencer, 124.
Loring, Gen. Charles G., 197, 198.
    On the Boston Art Museum portrait, 197.
Lucas, John, his examination of the body of Katharine Parr, 6.
Lucy, Sir Thomas, 124.
Lumley Castle, 192, 194.
Lumley, Lord, 192, 194.

Lumley portrait, 192.
    Its history, 192.
    Purchased by the Baroness Burdett-Coutts, 193.
    Resemblance of, to the Chandos portrait, 194.
    Vincent Brooks' chromo-lithograph of the, 195.
Luther, Martin, 93, 99.
    Mask of, 110.
Lysistratus of Sicyon, 109, 110.

MACBETH, Sir William D'Avenant's edition of, 173.
Mainz, 93.
Malone, Edmond, 26, 27, 77, 125, 155, 182, 184, 201.
    Advised that the Stratford bust should be painted white, 26.
    His statement regarding the date of Jansen's arrrival in England, 125.
    Ozias Humphry's drawing of the Chandos portrait made for, 77.
    The picture which he believed was by Jansen, 125.
Manchester, 213, 223.
Marshall's copy of the Droeshout engraving, 59.
    Copies of, in Boaden's *Inquiry*, and Wivell's *Inquiry*, 66.
    Delattre's engraving of, 66.
    H. Adlard's engraving of, 66.

INDEX.

Mashall's copy of the Droeshout, H. Robinson's engraving of, 66.
    The engraving of, in Johnson and Steevens' editions of Shakespeare, 1778, and 1785, 66.
Martin, D., his engraving of the Roubiliac statue, 234.
Mary, daughter of Edward IV., her tomb opened, 5.
    Effigy of, 111.
Mary of Scotland, Queen, her portrait painted by Zucchero, 204.
Mask, Death, see Death Mask.
Mask of Luther, 110.
Mask of Tasso, 110.
Masks, art of making, known very early, 109.
    How they are made, 105.
    Pliny on the art of making, 109.
Matthews, Jeremiah, his offer for the Stratford portrait, 162.
Maurer, J., his engraving of the Monument in Westminster Abbey, 230.
Mayence, 93, 94, 96, 98, 100, 101.
Measures of the Death Mask and the Stratford bust, 114.
Melanchthon, 93, 99.
Melbourne, 112.
Memphis, 111.
Merchant of Venice, 163.
Middle Scotland Yard, 208.
Midelburg, 124.
Milton, John, 173.

Milton, John, search for his remains, 10.
Monument in Westminster Abbey, 230.
    B. Holl's engraving of the, 231.
    Description of, 230.
    Dubose's engraving of the, 231.
    Halpin's engraving of the, 231.
    H. Gravelot's engravings of the, 231.
    J. Maurer's engraving of the, 230.
    Photographs of not satisfactory, 231.
    Rothwell's engraving of the, 231.
    The head of, somewhat like the Chandos portrait, 230.
Monuments, the faces of, made from masks, 110.
Müller, Professor, 94, 98, 100, 104.
    His letter to Ludwig Becker, 98.
Mummies, Egyptian, 111.
Museum of Fine Arts, Boston, 197.

NACK, 100, 101.
Napoleon I., 118.
Nash, Rev. Tredway, report of, on examination of Katharine Parr's remains, 7.
Nashe, Thomas, his grave, 2.
Neagle, J., his engraving of the Felton portrait, 150.
    His engraving of the Stratford bust, 38.
Nebuchadnezzar, 111.
Nelson, effigy of, 111.
New Place, 156, 233.
New Shakespeare Society, their chromophototype of the Stratford bust, 44.

New Shakespeare Society, their photograving of the Droeshout, 66.
    Their phototype of the Stratford bust, 44.
New Turnstile, 220.
Nichol, G., 144, 145.
Nicol, Nicholl, or Nicholls, his ownership of the Chandos portrait, 69, 70.
Niessen, J., his portrait from the Death Mask, 121.
    Photographs of his portrait from the Death Mask, 121.
Norwich, 206, 207.
Norwich portrait, 207.
Nose of the Stratford bust, shortness of the, 33.

O'CONNELL, J., owns the O'Connell portrait, 210.
O'Connell, portrait, 210.
    Description of the, 210.
    Exhibited in 1884 at the "Shakespeare Show," 210.
    Friswell on the, 210.
Old Green Dragon, 208.
Old Knowell, the Droeshout engraving supposed to represent Shakespeare as, 51.
Opening of Shakespeare's grave, 1.
Orford, Lord, 144.
Otis, Mrs. Harrison Gray, 197.
Otway, John, 69.

Owen, Professor, 112, 174, 176.
Oxford Street, 216.

PAGE, R., his engravings of the Jansen portrait, 137, 138.
Page's bust, crayon drawing of, 120.
    Photographs of, 120.
Page, William, always had the greatest faith in the Death Mask, 119.
    His bust from the Death Mask, 120.
    His portrait from the Death Mask, 121.
    Made masks from the Death Mask, 119.
    On the appearance of the left eye of the Death Mask, 115.
    On the Chandos portrait, 78.
    On the Halliwell-Phillipps copy of the Droeshout engraving, 55.
    On the indentation over the right eyebrow of the Death Mask, 113.
    On the similarity of the measures of the Death Mask and the Stratford bust, 114.
    On the Stratford bust, 30.
    Visited Darmstadt, 119.
Pall Mall, 232.
Parr, Katharine, Queen to Henry VIII., her tomb examined, 6.
Parr, N., his engraving of the Chandos portrait, 86.
Parry, James, 218.
Paxton, Sir Joseph, 176.

258   INDEX.

Photograph of the Boston Art Museum portrait, 197, 198.
  Of Charles Turner's mezzotint of the Jansen portrait, 138.
  Of Shakespeare, 4, 19.
  Of the Death Mask, 121.
Photographs of the Droeshout engraving, 64, 65.
  Of Monument in Westminster Abbey not satisfactory, 231.
  Of the Droeshout engraving not generally successful, 64.
  Of the Stratford bust, 42, 43, 44.
  Of the Stratford portrait, 156, 163, 164.
Photograving of the Droeshout engraving, 66.
Photo-lithographic copies of the Droeshout engraving, 64, 65.
Photo-zincographic copy of the Droeshout engraving, 64.
Picart, C., his engraving of the Droeshout, 62.
Piercy, W. F. Zincke originally bought the Winstanley portrait from, 225.
Pliny, on the art of making masks, 109.
Pope, Alexander, 185.
Preston, his photograph of the Chandos portrait, 92.
Prince Rupert, his reputed ownership of the Jansen portrait, 131.

QUEEN Anne, effigy of, 111.
  Queen Elizabeth, effigy of, 111.
Queen Mary, effigy of, 111.
Queen Mary of Scotland, her portrait painted by Zucchero, 204.

RABONE, John, his copy of the Stratford portrait, 156.
Radclyffe, E., his engraving of the Stratford bust, 41.
Raphael, 180.
  His tomb examined, 10.
Raye, Sir John Lister, paid four hundred pounds for the Zoust portrait, 203.
Reading, Burnet, his engraving of the Shakespeare Gallery Alto Relievo, 233.
Restoration of the Stratford bust by Collins, 26.
Review, the Critical, 127, 128.
Reynolds, Sir Joshua, 202.
  His opinion of the Chandos portrait, 75.
  Made a copy of the Chandos portrait, 72.
Ribet, cleaned the Talma portrait and afterwards restored it, 228.
Richardson, William, 141, 148.
  His proposals for the publication of engravings of the Felton portrait, 148.
Rippon, George, 193.
Rivers, his engraving of the Droeshout, 61.
Robinson, E. W., his drawing of the Stratford bust, 42.

Robinson, H., his engraving of Marshall's copy of the Droeshout, 66.
　His engraving of the Chandos portrait, 89.
　His engraving of the Droeshout, 63.
　His engraving of the Jansen portrait, 138.
　His engraving of the Stratford bust, 42.
Rockwood, his photograph of the Ward statue, 235.
Rodd, H., on Richard Burbage's portrait at Dulwich College, 72.
　On the Chandos portrait, 76.
Rohrbach, P., his lithograph of the Chandos portrait, 92.
Rothwell, his engraving of the Monument in Westminster Abbey, 231.
Roubiliac, Lewis Francis, 234.
Roubiliac statue, 234.
　Description of the, 234.
　D. Martin's engraving of the, 234.
　W. Holl's engraving of the, 234.
　The face somewhat like the Chandos portrait, 234.
Rowe's edition of Shakespeare, contained engraving of the Stratford bust, 36.
Rupert, Prince, his reputed ownership of the Jansen portrait, 131.
Ruperts, 131.

SANDRART, *Academiæ Picturæ Nobilis*, 123.

Sawyer, R., his engraving of the Droeshout, 61.
Scarborough, Earl of, 192.
Schaaffhausen, Dr. Hermann, 95.
　On ancient effigies, 111.
Scharf, George, on the Chandos portrait, 75, 80.
Schiller, his tomb opened, 9.
Schön, Martin, 93, 99.
Scotland Yard, Middle, 208.
Scott, Sir Walter, his large upper lip, 35.
　On the Stratford bust, 35.
Scott, T. D., his drawing of the Chandos portrait, 91.
　His drawing of the Stratford bust, 41.
Scriven, E., his engraving of the Chandos portrait, 88, 90.
　His engraving of the Stratford bust, 40.
Seldon, John, 227.
Shakespeare Gallery, 232.
Shakespeare Gallery Alto Relievo, 232.
　B. Holl's engraving of the, 233.
　B. Smith's engraving of the, 233.
　Burnet Reading's engraving of the, 233.
　Designed and executed by J. Banks, 232.
　Girtin and Scriven's engraving of the, 233.
　James Stow's engraving of the, 233.
　S. Rawle's engraving of the, 233.
　The face of the, resembles George Washington, 233.

260 INDEX.

Shakespeare Gallery Alto Relievo, Vitalba's engraving of the, 233.
    W. Humphry's engraving of the, 233.
Shakespeare's grave, 2.
Shakespeare Show, 191, 210.
Sharp, W., his engraving of the Dunford portrait, 223.
Sherburn Castle, 124.
Sherwin, W., his engraving of the Droeshout, 60.
Shylock, the Chandos portrait supposed to represent Shakespeare as, 82.
Simon, I., his mezzotint of the Zoust portrait, 201.
Skull of Shakespeare, the great good it would accomplish, 13.
Skulls of saints, preserved in portrait-busts in Christian churches, 111.
Smirke, Robert, his picture of Stratford bust, 39.
Smith, B., his engraving of the Shakespeare Gallery Alto Relievo, 233.
Smith, Edward, his engraving of the Chandos portrait, 89.
Smith, H. Wright, his engraving of the Felton portrait, 152.
Smith, W., 219.
Smith, William, on the Halliwell-Phillipps copy of the Droeshout engraving, 54.
Soest (Zoust), 201.
Somerset, Duchess of, 132.
Somerset, Duke of, 130, 168.
Somerset portrait, the, 122.

Somerville, 182, 185.
Somerville, Lord, 183.
Sonrel, his photographs of the Boston Art Museum portrait, 197, 198.
Southampton, Earl of, 124.
Southampton family, 189.
South Kensington, 191.
Spelman, Henry, 227.
Spencer, Lord, 124.
Spode, 173.
Spurzheim, Dr., on the Stratford bust, 34.
Stace, Machell, 208, 209.
Stace portrait, 208.
    Description of the, 208.
    History of the, 208.
    Robert Cooper's engraving of the, 209.
    W. Holl's engraving of the, 209.
Starling, his engraving of the Stratford bust, 41.
Steevens, George, 141, 143, 144, 145, 147, 148, 149.
    Believed that the Felton portrait was the original of the Droeshout engraving, 51.
    On the Chandos portrait, 77.
    On the Droeshout engraving, 48.
    Owned a copy of the Felton portrait painted by J. Boydell, 147.
St. Erasmus, Chapel of, 110.
St. George's Chapel, Windsor, 5.
St. Luke's Church, 204.
Storm, G. F., his engraving of the Ashborne portrait, 170.

INDEX.   261

Stow, James, his engraving of the Shakespeare Gallery Alto Relievo, 233.
Stratford bust, 21, 116, 119, 120, 178, 200.
   A. Birrell's engraving of the, 38.
   A stone pen originally in the right hand of the, 35.
   Benjamin West on the, 34.
   Boaden on the, 29.
   Comparison of, with the Death Mask, 116.
   Condition of in 1814, 33.
   Description of the, 24.
   Difference in appearance of, when colored, 27.
   Disappointing to most people, 35.
   Dr. C. M. Ingleby on the, 29.
   Dr. Spurzheim on the, 34.
   E. Radclyffe's engraving of the, 41.
   Engraving of, in Rowe's edition of Shakespeare, 36.
   E. Scriven's engraving of the, 40.
   E. W. Robinson's drawing of the, 42.
   F. Eginton's engraving of the, 38.
   Forefinger and thumb broken off the, 26.
   Francis Holl's engraving of the, 42.
   Friswell on the, 28.
   From a cast after death, 33.
   Fry's engraving of the, 40.
   F. W. Fairholt on the, 32.
   F. W. Fairholt's engraving of the, 41.
   George Bullock made a cast of the, in 1814, 33.
   G. Vertue's engraving of the, 37.
   Stratford bust, G. Greatbach's engraving of the, 41.
   Grignion's engraving of, 38.
   Had become dilapidated in 1749, 25.
   H. Gravelot's engraving of the, 37.
   H. Robinson's engraving of the, 42.
   Inscription under the, 24.
   I. S. Agar's engraving of the, 40.
   Its appearance different when viewed from various positions, 36.
   J. Boaden's drawing of the, 40.
   J. Boydell's engraving of the, 38.
   J. Neagle's engraving of the, 38.
   John Bell thought it was from a mask, 33.
   J. Thurston's drawing of the, 39.
   Length of upper lip of the, 33.
   Malone advised that it should be painted white, 26.
   New Shakespeare Society's chromophototype of the, 44.
   New Shakespeare Society's phototype of the, 44.
   Photographs of the, 42, 44.
   Poorness of the eyes of the, 33.
   Possesses no claims to be regarded as a work of art, 36.
   Probably erected by Shakespeare's family shortly after his death, 35.
   R. Ashby's engraving of the, 39.
   R. B. Wheler stated that there was no date or inscription on the back of the, 34.

262 INDEX.

Stratford bust, resemblance of the Burn portrait to the, 191.
    Resemblance of the moustache of the Boardman miniature to that of the, 207.
    Resemblance of the Stratford portrait to the, 157, 158, 161.
    Restoration of the, 26.
    Robert Smirke's picture of the, 39.
    Rudely cut, 18, 36.
    Samuel Ireland's engraving of the, 38.
    Sculptured from a mask, 103.
    S. Harding's drawing of the, 38.
    Shortness of nose of the, 33.
    Similarity of the measures of, to the Death Mask, 115.
    Sir Francis Chantrey thought it was from a mask, 33.
    Starling's engraving of the, 41.
    T. A. Dean's engraving of the, 40.
    T. D. Scott's drawing of the, 41.
    The Droeshout engraving as well authenticated as the, 50.
    The Hardie portrait resembles the, 213.
    The white paint on the, removed by Collins, 26.
    Thrupp's photographs of the, 43.
    W. Finden's engraving of the, 39.
    Wheler's drawing of the, 38.
    William Page on the, 30.
    William Ward's engraving of the, 39.
    Wivell on the, 30.

Stratford bust, Wivell's drawing of the, 40.
    W. J. Linton's engraving of the, 42.
    W. T. Fry's engraving of the, 39.
    W. Wallis' engraving of the, 41.
Stratford Church, 155.
Stratford portrait, 153.
    Charles Wright on the, 160.
    Cleaned by Simon Collins, 153.
    Discovery of the, 153.
    Discovery of the, excited great interest, 157.
    History of the, as given in the circular given to visitors to Collins' studio, 154.
    Inscription on the fire-proof case in which it is kept, 163.
    Its great resemblance to the Stratford bust, 157, 158, 161.
    J. O. Halliwell-Phillipps on the, 160.
    John Rabone's copy of the, 156.
    Not the work of an artist of much ability, 162.
    Photographed after it was cleaned, 156.
    Photographs of the, 156.
    Presented to the town of Stratford by W. O. Hunt, 162.
    Purchased at a sale at the Clopton House, 153.
    Restored, 154.
    The Examiner on the, 161.
    The face covered with beard before it was cleaned by Simon Collins, 154.

Stratford portrait, the majority of writers have thought it was from the Stratford bust, 158.
    The offer of Jeremiah Matthews to purchase it, 162.
    Visit of the Birmingham Archæological Association to see the, 156.
Stratford-upon-Avon, 2, 20, 153, 154, 156, 158, 162, 164, 207, 233.
    Tercentenary celebration of Shakespeare's birth at, 112.
    The Death Mask exhibited at, in 1864, 112.
Streatham Street, 208.
Surgeons, College of, 174, 176.
Swaine, J., his engraving of the Droeshout, 61.
Sydenham, 175, 176.

TABLET, Hardiknutian, 145.
    Talma, bought the Talma portrait for one thousand francs, 229.
Talma portrait, 228.
    Bought by Allen, 228.
    Charles Lamb said to have fallen on his knees before it, and to have kissed it, 229.
    Cleaned by Ribet, 228.
    Forged by W. F. Zincke, 228.
    Formerly owned by W. H. Ireland, 228.
    History of the, 228.

Talma portrait, inscription on the, 229.
    Originally represented an old lady, 228.
    Sold after Talma's death for three thousand one hundred francs, 229.
    Sold by Foster, 228.
Tasso, mask of, 110.
Taylor, John, 70.
Taylor, Joseph, 68, 70.
Teddington, 201.
Tercentenary of Shakespeare's birth, 112, 193, 207.
Theatre, Globe, 196.
Thompson, John, his engraving of the Chandos portrait, 88.
Thomson, I., his engraving of the Felton portrait, 150.
Thoms, W. J., suggested that the Death Mask represented Cervantes, 118.
Three Pigeons, 208.
Thrupp, his photographs of the Stratford bust, 43.
Thurston, his drawing of the Droeshout, 61.
Thurston, John, his drawing of the Felton portrait, 150.
Thurston, J., his drawing of the Stratford bust, 39.
Tercentenary of Shakespeare's birth, 112, 193, 207.
Times, The, 160.
Timmins, Samuel, 168, 233.
Tomkins, P. W., his engraving of the Chandos portrait, 87.

Tonson, Jacob, copy of the Chandos portrait on the publications of, 85.
Triphook, 202.
Trotter, T., his engravings of the Felton portrait, 149.
Tuffing, 208.
Turner, Charles, his mezzotint of the Dunford portrait, 223.
    His mezzotint of the Jansen portrait, 137.
Twickenham, 201.

URSULA, Church, Golden Chamber of the, 112.
Ut magus, above Earlom's mezzotint of the Jansen portrait, 133.

VANDER Gucht, 84, 86, 130.
    G., his engraving of the Chandos portrait, 84, 86.
    His drawing of the Chandos portrait, 130.
Vander Gucht, M., his engraving of the Chandos portrait, 82.
Vansomer, Paul, 75, 224.
Vault, Shakespeare buried in a, 16.
Vertue, G., his engraving of the Chandos portrait, 84.
    His engraving of James I., 128.
    His engraving of the Stratford bust, 37.
Vitalba, his engraving of the Shakespeare Gallery Alto Relievo, 233.

Von Brandenburg, Albrecht, 93, 99.
Von Kesselstadt, Francis, 93, 94, 95, 96, 97, 99, 100, 101, 102, 103, 104.
    His collection of pictures, 93.

WAAGEN, Dr., 72, 187.
    His remarks on Dryden's copy of the Chandos portrait, 72.
Wallis, W., his engraving of the Stratford bust, 41.
Walpole, 124, 125.
Walpole's Anecdotes of Painting, 123.
Ward, J. Q. A., his statue, 235.
Ward statue, 235.
    Description of the, 235.
    Davis' engraving of the, 235.
    Rockwood's photograph of the, 235.
Ward, William, his engraving of Stratford bust, 39.
Warren, C., his engravings of the Felton portrait, 150.
Warwick Castle, 187.
Warwick portrait, 187.
    Description of the, 187.
    History of unknown, 187.
Washington, George, the face of the Shakespeare Gallery Alto Relievo resembles, 233.
Waters, Ralph, 193.
Webb, 189.
West, Benjamin, 34, 180, 221.
    On the Stratford bust, 34.

Westmacott, owned the Felton portrait, 145.
Westminster Abbey, 110.
    Description of the Monument in, 230.
West Smithfield, 199.
Wheler, R. B., 155.
    His drawing of the Stratford bust, 38.
    Stated that there was no date or inscription on the back of the Stratford bust, 34.
William, effigy of, 111.
William III., 180.
William IV., 179.
Wilson, J., 142, 143, 144.
    His account of the history of the Felton portrait, 142.
    On the Jennings miniature, 190.
    The account he gave Steevens of the Felton portrait, 143.
Windsor, St. George's Chapel, 5.
Winstanley portrait, 224.
    Description of the, 224.
    Forged by W. F. Zincke, 225.
    History of the, 224.
    Inscription under the, 225.
Winstanley, Thomas, 224, 225.
Wivell, Abraham, 30, 40, 88, 89, 131, 133, 146, 147, 152, 155, 190, 201, 202, 203, 213, 217, 218, 219, 227.
    Applied to Holder for information concerning the Dunford portrait, 219.
    Ascertained that the Dunford portrait was a forgery by Edward Holder, 218.

Wivell, Abraham, discovered that the Hardie portrait was forged by Zincke, 213.
    Found J. Boydell's copy of the Felton portrait, 147.
    His drawing of the Chandos portrait, 88, 89.
    His drawing of the Stratford bust, 40.
    His engraving of the Felton portrait, 152.
    His statement concerning the panel on which the Jansen portrait is painted, 133.
    His statement that *Ut magus* is not on the Jansen portrait, 133.
    His visit to Samuel Woodburn, 131.
    On the Droeshout engraving, 48.
    On the Felton portrait, 147.
    On the Jennings miniature, 190.
    On the Stratford bust, 30.
    Purchased the Zincke portrait, 227.
Wolsey, Cardinal, 179.
Woodburn, 130, 131, 132.
    His purchase of the Jansen portrait for the Duke of Hamilton, 130, 131.
Wood-cuts of the Droeshout engraving, 66.
Wornum, Ralph N., his edition of Walpole's *Anecdotes of Painting*, 123.
Worthington, W. H., his engraving of the Droeshout, 62.
Wright, Charles, 159, 160.
    On the Stratford portrait, 160.
Wright, T., his engraving of the Jansen portrait, 138.

Wright, T., his ownership of the Zoust portrait, 201.
Wriothesley, Elizabeth, 124.

ZINCKE portrait, 226.
  Description of the, 226.
  Purchased by Wivell, 227.
  W. Holl's engraving of the, 227.
Zincke, W. F., 213, 220, 225, 226, 227, 228.
  Forged the Hardie portrait, 213.
  Forged the Talma portrait, 228.
  Forged the Winstanley portrait, 225.
  Painted the Zincke portrait, 227.
Zoust, his earliest picture in England, 201.
Zoust portrait, 201.
  Description of the, 202.
  I. Simon's mezzotint of the, 201.
  Lionel Booth has a copy of the, 203.
  Owned by T. Wright, 201.

Zoust portrait, Sir John Lister Raye paid four hundred pounds for the, 203.
  W. Holl's engraving of the, 203.
Zuccaro, Federigo, (Zucchero,) 196.
Zucchero, 197, 198, 204, 205.
  Compelled to leave England, 204.
  Painted portraits of Queen Elizabeth and Queen Mary, 204.
  The Boston Art Museum portrait could not have been painted by, if it represents Shakespeare, 198.
Zucchero portrait, 204.
  Could not have been painted by Zucchero, if it represents Shakespeare, 204.
  Description of the, 205.
  Henry Green's mezzotint of the, 205.
  The eyes very singular, 205.
  Thought by Boaden to resemble Torquato Tasso, 205.
  W. Holl's engraving of the, 205.

www.ingramcontent.com/pod-product-compliance
Lightning Source LLC
Chambersburg PA
CBHW022107290426
44112CB00008B/578